New Cottage Style

A *Sunset* Design Guide

by Allison Serrell and the Editors of *Sunset*

Contents

Welcome to the New Cottage Style. Before you start wondering what techniques or trends are involved, rest assured this decorating approach is a breeze to pull off. It's all about creating fresh, clutter-free spaces that are warm and livable. There aren't any fussy rules to follow, just a wealth of inspiration and expert ideas to really make your home shine.

On the pages of this guide, we'll show you spaces that are clean-lined and comfortable. You'll see calming rooms created with soft, neutral palettes, lots of natural materials, time-honored furnishings, and singular personal accents. Our panel of design experts from around the country will take you through the process of creating these cozy, serene spaces as they suggest ways to lighten and brighten your home while infusing warmth throughout. Enjoy.

©2011 by Time Home Entertainment Inc.
135 West 50th Street, New York, NY 10020

ISBN-13: 978-0-376-01356-9
ISBN-10: 0-376-01356-7
Library of Congress Control
Number: 2011925914

10 9 8 7 6 5 4 3 2 1
First Printing July 2011
Printed in the United States of America

OXMOOR HOUSE
VP, *Publishing Director:* Jim Childs
Editorial Director: Susan Payne Dobbs
Brand Manager: Fonda Hitchcock
Managing Editor: Laurie S. Herr

SUNSET PUBLISHING
President: Barb Newton
VP, Editor-in-Chief: Katie Tamony
Creative Director: Mia Daminato
Art Director: Jim McCann

New Cottage Style:
A Sunset Design Guide
CONTRIBUTORS
Author: Allison Serrell
Managing Editor: Bridget Biscotti Bradley
Photo Editor: Philippine Scali
Production Specialist: Linda M. Bouchard
Proofreader: John Edmonds
Indexer: Marjorie Joy
Series Designer: Vasken Guiragossian

To order additional publications, call 1-800-765-6400

For more books to enrich your life, visit **oxmoorhouse.com**

Visit Sunset online at **sunset.com**

For the most comprehensive selection of Sunset books, visit **sunsetbooks.com**

For more exciting home and garden ideas, visit **myhomeideas.com**

Cover Photo: Thomas J. Story

4

Design Panel

The following design professionals from across the United States lent their enormous talent and valuable advice to the pages of this book.

Mina Brinkey
BLOGGER

Mina Brinkey writes and edits Bohemian Vintage, a website and blog she launched in 2007 that brings design ideas, product reviews, and personal stories to thousands of readers each month. Mina lives in Tampa Bay, Florida, and has been featured in various publications, including *The Tampa Bay Times* and *Apartment Therapy*. Mina also runs an online boutique on www.etsy.com specializing in vintage treasures.
www.bohemianvintageonline.com

Austin Harrelson
INTERIOR DESIGNER

Austin Harrelson is best known for his unique interpretation of classic design. The Miami-based designer, who has been creating beautiful spaces for the past 12 years, was listed among *House Beautiful*'s "America's Top Young Designers" in 2003. Setting himself apart from other designers, Austin gets heavily involved in the construction process, as he feels that it is the groundwork for great design. His work includes recently finished projects in New York City, Ocean Reef, St. Martin, and La Gorce Island, Miami Beach. He studied sculpture and design at the School of Visual Arts in New York.
www.austinharrelson.com

Liz Williams
INTERIOR DESIGNER

Liz Williams is an Atlanta native and holds a BFA in interior design from Georgia State University. In 1998 she launched Liz Williams Interiors, a full-service interior design firm in Atlanta specializing in classic living spaces. Incorporating a balanced mix of traditional and contemporary design elements with fresh ideas, Liz works closely with clients to create timeless spaces that are as comfortable as they are elegant. Her work has been published in *Atlanta Homes and Lifestyles*, *Better Homes and Gardens*, *Cottage Style*, and *Décor*. | **www.lizwilliamsinteriors.com**

Alisha Peterson and Susan Delurgio
INTERIOR DESIGNERS

After many years of working in the design and retail fields, Alisha and Susan decided in 2006 to combine their talents to launch Beach House Style, a lifestyle shop in Marin County, California, that also offers full-design services. The business was created with the idea that living spaces should exude a carefree sensibility and that one's home should be a comfortable and casual place of inspiration and relaxation. Beach House Style has been featured in *Sunset* magazine, *Coastal Living,* and *Better Homes and Gardens.* Alisha and Susan were also honored to be the 2007 interior design team for *Sunset* magazine's Summer Idea House. **www.mybeachhousestyle.com**

Paula Smail
DESIGNER

A self-taught textile designer and interior stylist, Paula is the owner of Henry Road, a Los Angeles-based design studio and store selling textiles, home goods, and gifts. One of her childhood homes was a house on Henry Road in South Africa. Since leaving there, she has traveled extensively and includes London, Paris, and New York in the long list of places she has lived. Paula's style is a happily eclectic mix of color, eras and ethnicities fueled by a life spent rearranging furniture, scouring flea markets all over the world, and reading piles of design magazines. | **www.henryroad.com**

Molly Wood
LANDSCAPE DESIGNER

Molly Wood's earliest childhood memories are of sitting by a creek in Ashland, Oregon, building rock pools for her dolls to play in. "Nature is my playground and has been my inspiration from day one," she says. After studying art and design at the Academy of Arts in San Francisco, Molly moved to Laguna Beach, California, where she worked in a nursery and maintained private gardens. In 1995 she launched Molly Wood Garden Design in Costa Mesa, California, a full-service landscape design firm that also offers one-of-a-kind outdoor furniture and accessories. | **www.mollywoodgardendesign.com**

Bill Ingram
ARCHITECT

After graduating from Auburn University with a degree in architecture in 1983, Bill Ingram settled in Birmingham, where he runs a private firm designing houses throughout the Southeast as well as around the country. His work has been featured in *Southern Accents, House and Garden, Veranda, House Beautiful,* and *Cottage Living.* **www.billingramarhcitect.com**

Tracey Rapisardi
INTERIOR DESIGNER

Tracey Rapisardi has been an interior designer for 25 years. As a child growing up on the New England coast, Tracey experienced true cottage living, which significantly shaped her own design style. Her projects, which have taken her up and down the East Coast from Maine to Florida, have been featured in more than 50 magazines and books, including *Coastal Living, Traditional Home, Better Homes and Gardens, Creative Home, Cottage Style, Beautiful Homes,* and *Beach Houses.* Tracey

designed the 2008 *Coastal Living* Idea Cottage and recently moved her interior design business from Portland, Maine, to Sarasota, Florida. **www.searosedesigns.com**

> "Cottage style reflects a simpler way of living."
> —Tracey Rapisardi, interior designer

BELOW LEFT In a room with strong architectural elements like wood paneling and beamed ceilings, keep furnishings simple and neutral.

BELOW RIGHT Wood countertops and flooring, a farmhouse sink, white painted cabinets, and cheerful plaid window treatments combine to create a homey feel in this bright, inviting kitchen.

RIGHT Painted wood evokes true cottage style. A coat of white paint on wood floors, doors, and furnishings softens a room.

Replace your rocking chairs with modern canvas fold-outs for sundown gatherings on the porch.

> "Cottage style reflects
> a simpler way of living."
> —Tracey Rapisardi, interior designer

BELOW LEFT In a room with strong architectural elements like wood paneling and beamed ceilings, keep furnishings simple and neutral.

BELOW RIGHT Wood countertops and flooring, a farmhouse sink, white painted cabinets, and cheerful plaid window treatments combine to create a homey feel in this bright, inviting kitchen.

RIGHT Painted wood evokes true cottage style. A coat of white paint on wood floors, doors, and furnishings softens a room.

Paula Smail
DESIGNER

A self-taught textile designer and interior stylist, Paula is the owner of Henry Road, a Los Angeles-based design studio and store selling textiles, home goods, and gifts. One of her childhood homes was a house on Henry Road in South Africa. Since leaving there, she has traveled extensively and includes London, Paris, and New York in the long list of places she has lived. Paula's style is a happily eclectic mix of color, eras and ethnicities fueled by a life spent rearranging furniture, scouring flea markets all over the world, and reading piles of design magazines. | www.henryroad.com

Alisha Peterson and Susan Delurgio
INTERIOR DESIGNERS

After many years of working in the design and retail fields, Alisha and Susan decided in 2006 to combine their talents to launch Beach House Style, a lifestyle shop in Marin County, California, that also offers full-design services. The business was created with the idea that living spaces should exude a carefree sensibility and that one's home should be a comfortable and casual place of inspiration and relaxation. Beach House Style has been featured in *Sunset* magazine, *Coastal Living,* and *Better Homes and Gardens.* Alisha and Susan were also honored to be the 2007 interior design team for *Sunset* magazine's Summer Idea House.
www.mybeachhousestyle.com

Bill Ingram
ARCHITECT

After graduating from Auburn University with a degree in architecture in 1983, Bill Ingram settled in Birmingham, where he runs a private firm designing houses throughout the Southeast as well as around the country. His work has been featured in *Southern Accents, House and Garden, Veranda, House Beautiful,* and *Cottage Living.*
www.billingramarhcitect.com

Molly Wood
LANDSCAPE DESIGNER

Molly Wood's earliest childhood memories are of sitting by a creek in Ashland, Oregon, building rock pools for her dolls to play in. "Nature is my playground and has been my inspiration from day one," she says. After studying art and design at the Academy of Arts in San Francisco, Molly moved to Laguna Beach, California, where she worked in a nursery and maintained private gardens. In 1995 she launched Molly Wood Garden Design in Costa Mesa, California, a full-service landscape design firm that also offers one-of-a-kind outdoor furniture and accessories. | www.mollywoodgardendesign.com

Tracey Rapisardi
INTERIOR DESIGNER

Tracey Rapisardi has been an interior designer for 25 years. As a child growing up on the New England coast, Tracey experienced true cottage living, which significantly shaped her own design style. Her projects, which have taken her up and down the East Coast from Maine to Florida, have been featured in more than 50 magazines and books, including *Coastal Living, Traditional Home, Better Homes and Gardens, Creative Home, Cottage Style, Beautiful Homes,* and *Beach Houses.* Tracey designed the 2008 *Coastal Living* Idea Cottage and recently moved her interior design business from Portland, Maine, to Sarasota, Florida.
www.searosedesigns.com

Chapter 1

Elements of New Cottage Style

What is the New Cottage Style? Unlike other approaches to decorating, it isn't dictated by a lot of rules. Cottage style has always been relaxed and casual. It's versatile and easy to maintain, like a comfy slipcovered couch. Above all, cottage style is clean and uncluttered, so rooms feel fresh instead of fussy. Simple, solid furnishings, natural materials, and lots of personal accents are the essence of the look. Today, the style is updated with modern touches. You'll see open, airy spaces defined by clean-lined furnishings and a subdued palette. So relax, make a pot of tea, and put your feet up. The photographs and expert advice on these pages are sure to inspire you.

Cottage living spaces emphasize natural elements like wooden furnishings and sea grass rugs. Paint a brick fireplace white to lighten the room and make an above-the-mantel display pop.

ABOVE A time-worn cottage beckons visitors year after year.

RIGHT Paint double patio doors blue for a touch of French country cottage style.

OPPOSITE PAGE An attic or dormer room can be a cozy bedroom retreat. The ceiling and upper walls are painted a sky blue for a tranquil feel.

"Looking at the light outside is my way of marking time."

—Molly Wood, landscape designer

LEFT Exposed wood beams give cottage spaces a sense of history.

ABOVE A homey dining nook is warmed by vintage paintings and a cozy bench.

LEFT Furniture with history transforms a house into a home. A paint-flecked, worn wooden table is the soul of this casual kitchen.

OPPOSITE PAGE Personal touches humanize living spaces. Fill a living room wall with informal artwork and mirrors to project true cottage style.

"Cottage style shows the history of who is living there."

—Liz Williams, interior designer

ABOVE In a bathroom with white paneled walls, wood floors, and large windows, keep accessories to a minimum to show off the room's architectural bones.

RIGHT Vintage table linens have endless uses. Sturdy napkins can double as hand towels in the bathroom, and a tablecloth can drape a sofa for a layered, textural effect.

OPPOSITE PAGE Bright pinks and greens combined with a streamlined glass and metal coffee table bring a light, modern air to this traditional stone-walled cottage.

"Style can be found on any budget."

—Alisha Peterson, interior designer

"For a house to be great,
it ultimately has to be
super comfortable."

—Austin Harrelson,
interior designer

ABOVE Indoors or out, informal greenery displays pulled straight from the garden make you feel surrounded by nature.

LEFT Avoid heavy cabinetry in the kitchen. Open shelves lighten a room and add visual interest.

OPPOSITE PAGE In small bedrooms, versatile furnishings are a must. Here, a painted dresser doubles as a nightstand.

Wood floors painted in a checkerboard pattern were common in the early 20th century. Today painted wood floors give a room a finished look and a sense of history.

Choose one or two accent colors for your cottage bedroom. Here, multiple shades of brown and green echo nature's palette.

Vintage crossbar
faucets lend an old-
world look to a
contemporary sink,
while open shelves
and cabinets
emphasize the
casual vibe.

"Look at the potential in things you already have. If something has good bones, sometimes all it needs is a coat of paint."

—Mina Brinkey, blogger

ABOVE As an alternative to cabinetry, try freestanding furnishings and open shelves to create a homey, lived-in feeling in the kitchen. You needn't rely solely on harsh overhead kitchen illumination. Light from a small table lamp will give the room a warm glow.

Create an inviting, tactile atmosphere in the bathroom by combining contrasting textures.

In a paneled dining room, find a palette that works with wood. Here, a slate-colored farmhouse table and woven rush chairs complement the room's woodsy character.

LEFT Worn-wood and wicker furnishings with washable cushion covers turn this screened-in porch into a cozy indoor-outdoor room.

OPPOSITE PAGE Candles and throw pillows on the patio extend the casual cottage feel to outdoor gatherings.

"A cottage is a purely handcrafted house, one that a modest builder would have created from local materials."

—Bill Ingram, architect

Vintage furnishings, crisp white linens, and pale blue accents create a bright space that feels as though it's been just this way for decades.

ABOVE LEFT A welcoming entryway includes a place to hang your hats.

ABOVE RIGHT Wide horizontal stripes paired with a round vanity mirror evoke sea cabin vacations in a beach-side cottage.

RIGHT Mix and match textures for a unique display.

"Any single design aesthetic is too singular. A house should have an eclectic blend of things."

—Paula Smail, designer

Chapter 2

Kitchens and Dining Rooms

Kitchens, lighten up! We've become so accustomed to the turbocharged kitchen-as-command-center that we've neglected the heart in our hearths. Hulking ranges and roomfuls of cabinets are impressive but a bit foreboding. Your kitchen should nourish you and feed your senses, so bring it down to human scale. Make it a warm and welcoming space to spend time in with a comfortable eating area, lovely things to look at, and plenty of good taste. If you have a separate dining room, use it for more than formal dinner parties. Dining rooms are ideal for craft projects and homework, for extra storage, and as a quiet place to sit and read.

The chalkboard in this informal dining room keeps kids entertained and parents aware of play dates and grocery lists.

Defining the Space

Cottage kitchens are based on comfort and practicality, so think about how you actually use your kitchen and how to best adapt the space to your needs. Consider just how many hours you spend there, standing at the stove, chatting on the phone, paying bills. How do you use the space now and how would you like it to feel? Do you spend time at the kitchen table with your laptop? Is it a primary gathering spot for friends and family? Do you enjoy cooking daily? How big is your space and what are its assets and challenges? Large kitchens will benefit from distinct "zones" for food preparation, relaxing, and eating. If your kitchen is small and dark, suggests blogger Mina Brinkey, create the illusion of space and airiness by keeping to a white palette.

ABOVE In a large kitchen, use rugs, lighting fixtures, and furniture groupings to carve out distinct areas for food prep, eating, and relaxing.

OPPOSITE PAGE A striped cotton rug warms —and helps define—the food-prep zone of this cottage kitchen.

Eating Areas

If you have an eat-in-kitchen, you're likely spending even more time there. Banquets, benches, and nooks can all help create a lovely dining zone if space is at a premium. Positioned by a window, they become coveted spots to perch over coffee or a glass of wine. Warm the area with cushioned seating and soft, light window treatments.

If the flow of your space allows you to move easily from the kitchen to an adjoining breakfast nook or dining room, it will feel larger when flooring is kept continuous to unify the areas. You may wish to continue the kitchen color palette into the eating area, or change it up a bit with a slightly different wall hue, depending on whether you'd like the spaces to feel more separate or integrated.

Rugs can help define each zone and give the space a more finished look. If your space is large enough to accommodate a comfy seating area, don't hesitate to make one. There is nothing more luxurious than a kitchen with an overstuffed couch or a pair of deep-seated armchairs.

OPPOSITE PAGE, TOP A sturdy wooden table serves as a dining area and an extra surface for food preparation in this eat-in kitchen.

OPPOSITE PAGE, BOTTOM Make kitchen window seats as cozy as possible with cushions and an array of throw pillows. Keep fabrics simple so the area doesn't overwhelm an already hectic room.

RIGHT A wood-and-white color scheme makes for a seamless transition from cooking to dining zone.

INTERIOR DESIGNERS ALISHA PETERSON AND SUSAN DELURGIO ON

The Elements of a Cottage Kitchen

Focus on a few classic cottage features to give your kitchen added charm. **Wood floors** provide instant warmth. **Farmhouse sinks** are available in a wide variety of prices and sizes. **White cabinets** and **chunky open shelves** give a fresh cottage feel. **Glass storage containers** for grains and legumes add visual texture. **Wainscoting** on the walls has instant impact, as do **vintage appliances**. For warmth, use **cotton runners** or **durhi rugs**.

ABOVE LEFT A half wall visually separates the eating area beyond the kitchen without blocking the view.

ABOVE RIGHT This sunny breakfast nook feels like a solid part of the kitchen, thanks to detailed trim and molding around the windows and a built-in bench. An Arts and Crafts–style trestle table separates the bench and two light-weight aluminum chairs.

OPPOSITE PAGE White walls and cabinets, along with a wall of windows, make this kitchen with dark stained wood flooring and black countertops feel light and open.

Setting the Tone

Warm wooden furnishings, artwork on the wall, intimate lighting, and a blooming branch from the garden create an inviting atmosphere.

Because we spend so much time in our kitchens and dining spaces, they need to be functional, aesthetically pleasing, and, above all, *livable.* You needn't treat it as a simply utilitarian space. No matter your kitchen's size or shape, you can make it a welcoming space to spend time in. Does your kitchen have a comfortable place to sit? Is the lighting warm and pleasant? Are there interesting things to look at on the walls? You don't have to redo your whole kitchen to transform it; a few cottage touches—cozy furnishings, pleasing displays, and warm lighting— will provide plenty of character.

ABOVE Mix and match whites and earth tones in your table settings and napkins. Individual salt dishes make guests feel special.

RIGHT Dining by the hearth—be it a wood stove or fireplace—is one of life's greatest pleasures.

Flooring

Nothing matches the warmth of wood on kitchen floors. Wood provides texture and color and goes with any decor. The downside is that moisture causes wood to expand and contract, sometimes creating gaps between the planks. Wood may require some extra maintenance in the kitchen and show wear over time, but many people accept that as part of its charm. If you have a home with existing soft wood floors that need to be refinished, consider painting them a glossy white (or a slightly tinted hue), as was common in early-20th-century houses. To give your floors an especially historic look, choose reclaimed wood from older buildings that has been re-milled into tongue-and-groove planks. This is the best way to get instant patina, such as large knots, old nail holes, and deep cracks. Finish the flooring with a low-VOC polyurethane to protect it from water, or a natural oil, which is how floors were finished before the modern industrial age and which lets the beauty of the wood shine through.

Linoleum, a material commonly used in the early part of the 20th century, will also give your kitchen an authentic look. Linoleum is made of natural materials, including linseed oil, wood flour, tree resins, ground limestone, and natural pigments. It's extremely durable and comes in a wide array of colors and patterns. The classic black-and-white checked linoleum has a clean, graphic look that has never gone out of style. Whatever your flooring material, soften it with area rugs to warm the space and demarcate areas in your kitchen (consider one in front of the sink and one to define an eating area).

OPPOSITE PAGE
Made of natural materials, linoleum is extremely durable and easy to clean. A classic black-and-white checkerboard pattern will go with any color scheme.

TOP RIGHT Warm wood flooring offsets the chill of stainless-steel appliances. Wood floors show signs of wear over time, adding to their charm.

BOTTOM RIGHT Cork flooring is made of renewable materials and is soft enough that when you drop a glass, it likely will not break.

Appliances

This classic Aga stove has an appealingly old-fashioned look. Made in Britain, vintage Agas are usually left on continuously and keep the kitchen toasty warm.

Kitchen appliances have become almost like furniture, with a huge range of styles available, from vintage versions to professional-grade options.

On the whole, cottage kitchens are devoid of bells and whistles, so keep your appliances pared down to a human scale.

With so many possibilities on the market, it's easy to choose a range and refrigerator that perform well *and* look good. Standard black or white appliances or stainless-steel versions will go with just about any surrounding color or finish. If stainless leaves you cold, you can have the appliance paneled with woodwork to match your cabinets for a more integrated feel. You can even have it faced with chalkboard for a built-in message area.

ABOVE LEFT An antique 1905 stove, reclaimed-wood floors, and a large wooden table with surrounding stools add patina in this farmhouse kitchen.

TOP RIGHT A stove that is built into a corner of the kitchen can be a terrific space saver.

BOTTOM RIGHT Consider adding finished panels to your refrigerator and dishwasher that match your cabinets for an integrated look.

Vintage Ranges and Refrigerators

Refurbished vintage appliances, or those made to look old, have a charming retro style that has become quite popular. However, a restored antique Wedgewood or O'Keefe and Merritt stove is an expensive purchase. Vintage refrigerators may not be optimally efficient energy-wise, points out blogger Mina Brinkey. "Refrigerators are energy hogs," she says. Brinkey suggests opting for a new refrigerator (such as those made by Smeg) that comes in a 1950s color and style but is energy efficient. Either way, one or two vintage touches go a long way, so avoid an overly retro look or your kitchen may seem staged.

BLOGGER
MINA BRINKEY ON

Vintage Kitchen Accessories

For just a touch of vintage in the kitchen, check out local flea markets for retro dishes and glassware. Blue glass jars with old metal lids, a collection of vintage cake stands, milk glass plates, and rustic step stools can really make a statement.

These appliances look vintage but are brand-new models available in mod midcentury colors, adding instant pop. For a fun look suited to a casual beach house, play up the colors with coordinated tile, lighting, and accessories.

Sinks and Countertops

A large farmhouse sink like this soapstone example can be the showpiece of a cottage kitchen, especially when paired with basic subway tile and traditional face-frame cabinetry.

Kitchen sinks can make a strong statement, so consider your options carefully. Familiarize yourself with basic sink styles, such as drop-in (or overmount), undermount (where the sink sits below the countertop surface) integrated (where the sink is built of the same material as the countertop and fused to it), and apron or farmhouse sinks (set into a hole cut into the front edge of the counter, leaving the front edge exposed). Then decide how large a sink your space can accommodate and whether you want a single or double sink.

Farmhouse sinks are often made of classic soapstone or white porcelain, and they provide a classic touch that is ideal for a cottage kitchen. At a salvage yard, look for a vintage one that still shows potential, or purchase a new model.

ABOVE An under-mount sink allows you to sweep crumbs right off the countertop and into the basin. Wooden countertops have a timeless appeal.

LEFT This integrated sink, countertop, and backsplash were all cast in concrete. Wall-mounted faucets and an extra-long sink allow two people to do the dishes at the same time.

Countertops and Backsplashes

If possible, choose countertops made of natural materials that have been used for centuries, like stone or wood. Some porous stones such as marble will show signs of age over time, adding wonderful patina to your kitchen. Wood adds a wealth of warmth to the kitchen and will also show signs of wear but will last a lifetime if properly cared for. Stainless steel and single-color solid surfaces made of composite materials are more modern countertop options that can also work in cottage-style kitchens. For a classic backsplash that will go with most any countertop, use white subway tile that extends 4 inches up the wall, or to the bottom of your upper cabinets.

ABOVE LEFT Often used in restaurants, stainless-steel countertops are resistant to heat, water, rust and bacteria. Best of all, they are easy to clean.

ABOVE RIGHT Marble countertops and backsplashes lend old-world charm to kitchens. Marble is more porous than some other stones, so it must be kept sealed and will develop patina over time.

LEFT Solid-surface countertops can have integrated backsplashes for a simple, seamless aesthetic.

This soapstone farm-house sink blends into the surrounding countertop.

Worktables

Don't be afraid to mix worktable materials. These chunky butcher blocks set atop metal legs provide the authentic look of a working kitchen.

LEFT If your kitchen has the space, employ a large worktable around which friends and family can gather to help cook. A step stool is stored underneath for easy access.

BELOW Seamlessly coordinated with appliances, stainless-steel worktables are both practical and stylish. Wheels on the feet make it easy to move out of the way when not needed.

Having extra prep space—and a spot where your family and guests can gather informally—makes a kitchen especially inviting. Instead of a chunky island with cabinet doors and drawers, which can weigh the room down, consider a freestanding worktable. A worktable is like furniture in your kitchen and can be functional and decorative at the same time. Top it with butcher block, which does double duty as surface area and chopping block. A stone-topped table makes the room feel solid and elegant, while stainless steel provides a touch of industrial chic.

You needn't use a table designed solely for the kitchen. "An unexpected piece will inject the space with personality," says interior designer Austin Harrelson, who used an old Chinese table for a kitchen island. "Don't be afraid to use things you would use in a living room," he suggests. The table should be slightly higher than a dining table. Counter height is appropriate if you will use the area for a prep station. Keep a few tall stools nearby so friends can keep you company while you chop.

INTERIOR DESIGNER
LIZ WILLIAMS ON

Kitchen
Worktables

The character of an older worktable gives relief from all the cabinets. I like to mix materials such as an iron frame with marble on top. Keep it open below for storing large items.

OPPOSITE PAGE, TOP Metal stools fit perfectly under one side of the island, taking up no extra floor space when stowed.

OPPOSITE PAGE, BOTTOM LEFT This warm wooden food-prep table is low enough for someone to pull up a chair and sip morning coffee while looking out the window.

OPPOSITE PAGE, BOTTOM RIGHT Make eating at the kitchen island easier by extending the countertop on one side. This model provides some closed storage yet still has long legs, so it doesn't appear too heavy.

ABOVE When designing or shopping for your worktable, draw from existing materials in your kitchen. Here, a cherry-topped island matches the built-in cabinetry.

Storage and Display

Open shelves mean you'll never forget what you have. To style them attractively, group like items, colors, and shapes together.

Organizing a kitchen well will make it more attractive and functional. If you are planning a new kitchen or if you need to improve upon the usability of your existing kitchen, take inventory of all your goods, including the pots, pans, dishes, and canned foods that need to be put away. Then group like items together and store them close to where they will be used. Store seasonal items and plates you use only for guests in harder-to-reach areas.

To avoid the heaviness of too much cabinetry, open up the space. Nearly all the experts on our panel are in favor of incorporating open shelves. Reminiscent of early kitchens with freestanding furniture rather than built-in cabinetry, open shelves feel homey, offer great display, and allow easy access to every-day items like cereal bowls and coffee mugs. To play up the beauty of your shelves, use reclaimed wood with a noticeable grain or simply coat them in glossy white paint.

Open storage has many advantages in the kitchen. A rack for pots above the stove lets you survey your options easily and adds visible sparkle to the space. In a real cook's kitchen, it's a nice reminder of all the good food made there. Plate racks keep your daily rotation close at hand and add visual interest to the room.

Additionally, keep your cabinet facings light—the darker the cabinets, the heavier they feel. To break up the monotony of one color, use glass doors (frosted or not) for cabinets above the sink. If you have storage space elsewhere, you may wish to eschew upper cabinets altogether. This will open up the space and give it the feel of a regular room.

ABOVE Glass doors break up the monotony of cabinets and allow some room for creative display.

LEFT Rather than house beautiful silverware in a drawer, display it where you can see and enjoy it.

LEFT These base cabinets provide open and closed storage, plus a pop of red that beautifully highlights glassware.

OPPOSITE PAGE, TOP LEFT Treat your pantry shelves as you would a bookshelf or display case by placing decorative photos or objects here and there.

OPPOSITE PAGE, TOP RIGHT Vintage tins and packaging make gorgeous kitchen displays. Don't hesitate to pick them up at flea markets solely for their visual appeal.

OPPOSITE PAGE, BOTTOM LEFT To avoid having too many contrasting colors and typefaces, transfer oils and vinegars to clear bottles and add pretty labels in your own handwriting.

OPPOSITE PAGE, BOTTOM RIGHT Cottage kitchen shelves should look well-stocked but not crammed or busy. Fill them out by grouping like items together and keep nonmatching glassware or cups in closed cabinets.

ABOVE Old-fashioned kitchens didn't have built-in cabinetry. Mixing and matching vintage tables, shelves, and crates gives a modern space the same feeling.

OPPOSITE PAGE Having a work surface, display area, and open shelving in your pantry packs a lot of solutions into one small space.

Freestanding Storage and Pantries

Incorporating freestanding cupboards, hutches, and armoires adds richness to the space, suggests blogger Mina Brinkey. "If you bring elegance to the kitchen, using it won't feel like drudgery," she says. "It sets a precedent for you to keep the room looking nice." Choose warm wooden pieces that are functional and simply designed. Think of them as your kitchen "wardrobe," a place to store lovely table linens, treasured cookbooks, or elegant serving pieces.

Pantries are a terrific boon for kitchens. Treat them like rooms in themselves with appropriate lighting and fresh paint. In addition to boxes and cans of food, pantries can store extra serving plates and appliances that clutter up the main part of the kitchen. Your ability to see everything you have at once will help keep items organized.

INTERIOR DESIGNER
TRACEY RAPISARDI ON

Furniture in the Kitchen

Early-1900s kitchens had freestanding furniture, not walls of built-in cabinets. Freestanding pieces such as hutches, tables, and buffets have American cottage charm. Look for vintage options to add even more character to newer kitchens. Use a mix of open and closed pieces so the space doesn't get too heavy.

Styling Your Kitchen

Adding that extra pop or personal touch makes the kitchen a place that you—and others—want to spend time in. Plants, jars of fresh herbs, and artwork create a homey and cozy space.

"Have fun with kitchen towels and accessories," recommend interior designers Alisha Peterson and Susan Delurgio. "Hang a cute apron on the wall or display pretty dish towels on hooks to make a statement and bring in color." Peterson also recommends hanging one big art piece (or perhaps a chalkboard for kids) on the wall as a focal point.

Create homey-looking displays on your counters. A wooden tray filled with olive oils and vinegars, a large sculptural bowl with fruit or vegetables, or a favorite piece of art hung just above the counter gives the eye a place to settle. For infusions of color, blogger Mina Brinkey suggests setting out a vintage toaster or another small appliance in a festive hue. Colorful pottery such as Fiestaware also brightens the space.

ABOVE If you have a bright backsplash, style shelves simply with a minimum of competing color.

LEFT Don't hesitate to install a kitchen shelf or two purely for decorative reasons. This cup-and-coral display infuses the space with color and texture.

OPPOSITE PAGE Add color to the kitchen to echo the seasons or your mood. Brightly hued fruit and accessories can be changed out when it suits you.

Casual Dining Rooms

No need to deem your dining room "formal" even if you enjoy frequent entertaining. Guests feel most comfortable in looser, more casually arranged spaces. And when you are not eating there, it may be the space to sprawl with homework or family projects, so make it as usable as possible.

Furniture

The shape of your table will be dictated somewhat by the dimensions of the room. A rectangular table allows for easier conversation, while long, narrow tables have an old-fashioned elegance to them that is very appealing. Small circular tables make everyone feel included if they are kept to a manageable size, but once a round table is large enough to seat more than six people, it can be hard to hear guests during a dinner party.

Most experts on our panel advised mixing and matching the table and chairs for a more eclectic and interesting look. Wood is an ideal material, especially one with an interesting grain or patina. Find chairs that complement but offset the table a bit, so that not all the furniture blurs together. Blond wooden tables look lovely with white chairs, or pair a darker wooden table with a medium-toned wooden chair. The more dark wood you have, the heavier the room will feel, so try pairing a wooden table with wicker or cane chairs to add texture, suggests interior designer Liz Williams. Colorful mismatched chairs add a jolt of color to a blond wooden, glass, or white table.

ABOVE A wooden bench breaks up the monotony of matching chairs and adds cottage style.

RIGHT Bring in textural objects such as a vintage mirror or a spray of branches to add interest in a simple room.

OPPOSITE PAGE Keep casual dining rooms comfortable and eclectic with mixed and matched furniture instead of sets.

TOP RIGHT If you don't have a designated dining room, look for an unused corner or find space in a sunroom or on a back porch to create a one-of-a-kind dining area.

BOTTOM RIGHT Pair colorful, casual chairs with a solid wooden table for a touch of unexpected visual interest.

OPPOSITE PAGE An empty table looks stiff and formal. When it's not in use, style your dining room table with a casual display of flowers, vases, books, or a lamp.

LANDSCAPE DESIGNER
MOLLY WOOD ON

Natural Displays

I like to take a walk with the kids to collect flowers or branches. We bring them inside, put them in a vase, and create our own nature display à la Andy Goldsworthy! I display colorful flowers and fruit to mark specific seasons. For the holidays, I might use a bowl of red pomegranates. When spring appears, I might bring in buckets of daffodils and bowls of lemons.

To avoid the floating-in-space look of a dining table, anchor the area with a textural rug and a light fixture.

Creating Atmosphere

Ideally your dining room will be a place where friends and family can settle in for a comfortable couple of hours over dinner. That means chairs should be comfy and not stiff; lighting should be warm. Interior designer Liz Williams suggests one main lighting fixture above the table and a floor lamp for ambient lighting that will give the room a cozy feel.

To bring definition to the room, use a rug to anchor the seating area and offset it with a sideboard for storage and display.

In a subdued dining room with unified furnishings, a prominent modern light fixture can strike just the right style note.

Multipurpose Dining Rooms

In between gatherings, don't let dining rooms go unused. The table can become a work surface for art or sewing projects, bill paying, or catching up on email.

To get the most out of the space, keep some useful supplies close at hand. A sideboard is ideal for storage (designate half for alternative storage or line the shelves with interchangeable baskets). If space is at a premium, a small, attractive chest of drawers or roll-top desk will do the job. Keep bills, stamps, art supplies, extra pens, maps, and other bits you are likely to use stowed there for when you need them.

Dining rooms also make wonderful libraries and reading rooms, especially if you are a book lover with multiple volumes. Carve out a corner of the room, line a wall or two with shelves, and stock them with your favorite books. Place an overstuffed chair or two nearby, and you have a comfy nook for reading or sorting the mail. Keep coffee table books and other reference materials stacked on the dining room table, and make sure you have appropriate task lighting.

ABOVE LEFT Dining room tables were made for craft projects. Keep always-needed items like scissors, tape, pens, sewing kits, and paper stowed in the sideboard for easy access.

ABOVE RIGHT Set the dining room table in a festive fashion purely for display so you can enjoy the space even when guests aren't expected. The upholstered chair in the corner is situated near a window, creating a private reading nook.

OPPOSITE PAGE A dining room cabinet with a pullout work surface is ideal for paying bills, updating your calendar, or sorting mail.

Chapter 3

Living Rooms

It's time we put life back into our living rooms. After all, these are dynamic spaces, not static showrooms or tricked-out media centers. Your life unfolds here as you settle in with a magazine and a cup of coffee or catch up with friends over sloe gin fizzes. Above all, the room should feel warm and inviting, not forbidding. Natural materials will set the tone for a living, breathing space; an informal seating plan will energize the room. Living rooms need sofas you can sink into, not just perch on top of, so make comfort a priority. And remember, *you* are the essence of this space, so let it reflect your life and personality.

White walls and a grouping of vintage mirrors reflect the natural light in this cozy room with an eclectic mix of furnishings.

Defining the Space

Clean-lined wooden furnishings need not match or be of the same period. Mixing different styles with similar lines will add richness to the room. Choose one or two decorative pieces, such as these matching Asian cabinets, as the living room's focal point.

The seating area will be the hub of your living room. A couch usually defines this spot, but you can also anchor seating with two gloriously overstuffed chairs and a generous coffee table. First, find the optimal seating spot; it may be under a window, near bookcases or by a hearth. Try not to have your seating area face the doorway, as looking at this transitional space will feel busy, not calming.

Opt for informal, flexible seating plans that feel lived in and inviting. A couch surrounded by one or two comfortable armchairs, a stool or bench, and an ottoman or pouf provides flexibility and visual interest. Avoid static arrangements like two facing couches, as they may feel stiff instead of welcoming.

Open spaces feel inviting, so resist the urge to overcrowd your living room with furniture or too many things. "Cottage living means having only what you need and what you use," says architect Bill Ingram. Sometimes less really is more.

TOP RIGHT One or two graphic elements will make a room pop. Here, a striped rug and pillows add texture to the room's black-and-white color scheme.

BOTTOM RIGHT Make a small living room feel cozy and intimate with deep-seated chairs clustered around a soft rug.

ABOVE Instead of a couch, your seating plan may be defined by two chairs deep enough to curl up on. Time-worn leather creates a sense of history in the room.

LEFT To energize the space, create informal seating areas next to a sunny window.

RIGHT Place over-stuffed chairs with ottomans close together for an intimate seating area. Slipcovered furniture gives any room a cozy cottage look.

Furnishings

In a room rich with character, choose flexible, pared-down furnishings to anchor the space.

Gone are the days when no one dared enter the living room for fear of messing it up, so you needn't be too serious about your design. Most of the experts on our panel suggest you choose an eclectic mix of flexible, pared-down furnishings. "People often get too fixated on one style or one color and focus too much on matching," designer Paula Smail points out. Banish fussy, formal pieces. "Take out the preciousness," say interior designers Alisha Peterson and Susan Delurgio. "There is weight lifted when you de-clutter and simplify."

For visual interest that is not overpowering, mix and match textures and furnishing styles but keep room colors neutral and earthy.

DESIGNER
PAULA SMAIL ON

Editing Your Living Room

We accumulate so many things that we start not really seeing what we have. Schedule a "spring cleaning" day to solve this issue. Edit your furnishings by moving things around and paring down. Your living room should be flexible enough that you can change it for a fresh perspective.

Vintage Pieces

Ideally, your living room will have some furniture with history—a piece or two passed down from a family member or plucked from a flea market. Update where necessary. A 1940s chair, for example, will look handsome with contemporary upholstery or slipcovers. "Don't be afraid of chipping paint, unless you have small children, as the paint could have lead in it," interior designer Liz Williams says.

The patina of a vintage piece adds character and warmth. If you choose a leather chair, opt for an older one in an earthy brown that has faded with signs of wear. Overly dark, shiny leather can weigh a room down.

Use contrasting elements to achieve an eclectic mix. Unexpected juxtapositions give the room depth and texture, so go ahead and pair worn leather club chairs with a modern couch, or garden chairs with a midcentury table. Move things around until you come up with a compelling combination.

To anchor the room, choose a classic, well-made couch (one with a solid-wood frame) that will stand the test of time and mix with other pieces. A tuxedo or camel-back-style sofa will never look dated or trendy. From there, mix and match smaller furnishings that you love.

ABOVE Create visual contrast in your living room. Here, vintage leather club chairs and a rustic wooden coffee table look especially textural against white adobe walls.

OPPOSITE PAGE Pillows covered in vintage fabrics and a salvaged table and chair lend this room an appealing 1940s flair without making it seem too retro.

Coffee tables should look and feel solid but not heavy. Here, a lackluster vintage wooden chest is transformed into a pretty sculptural piece with a coat of glossy white paint.

Seating Areas

Armchairs and occasional chairs and tables help tie a seating area together. Wooden benches, too, are especially versatile. They can be piled with art books, or you can use them for extra seating or as a makeshift table. Scout yard sales or flea markets for graceful wooden benches with plenty of patina.

Coffee tables should be solid enough to put your feet on; avoid glass-topped or delicate versions if you are someone who likes to sprawl. Choose solid, natural materials like wood or bamboo. Oversized low tables (18 inches high or less) work as footstools and also let you stack books and magazines. Smaller tables placed next to the couch and chairs work well too; look for occasional stools that can double as tables.

Lighting

Living rooms should have a warm glow. To make the most of natural light, chose simple and informal window treatments. The nicer your windows look, the more they can be shown off. Ring-top curtains and billowy fabric panels create a casual look. Use a translucent fabric rather than something dense and heavy.

A mix of ambient, task, and accent lighting will provide enough versatility for entertaining or reading. Table lamps, especially, make a room feel warm. Keep table lamp designs simple and subdued. Check flea markets for one-of-a-kind versions (those in disrepair can be rewired if necessary).

> ### INTERIOR DESIGNER AUSTIN HARRELSON ON
>
> ## The Collected Look
>
> I like the contrast and juxtaposition of objects from different periods. You have to experiment with fancy things and junk—the mix makes it interesting. I like furniture to look collected, like it was slowly acquired over time.

TOP Simple solar shades play up the beauty of these sunny period windows. Smaller flexible pieces like poufs and side tables can be moved around to accommodate guests.

BOTTOM Carving out one main seating area, or a few smaller ones, by the hearth, near a window, or beside a cozy bookshelf brings context to the space.

Adding Texture

To make the living room especially warm and comfortable, layer plenty of textures. "If you don't have texture in the room, you have nothing," interior designer Austin Harrelson boldly maintains. Choose rugs, curtains, upholstery, pillows, and throws made of natural materials. Mix different fabrics and textiles for an added tactile quality. Drape sheepskins on your couch, and layer cotton rugs or kilims over a larger sea grass carpet. Offset a waxed wood floor with linen curtains. "It's the burlap with silk that humanizes a room," Harrelson points out.

Plants also add life to a living room. Play with scale and consider a larger tree-like plant to fill out a corner of the room, or use smaller, sculptural succulents in chunky white vases to anchor a seating area. Adorn your room with cut flowers and branches to reflect the seasons.

ABOVE LEFT An earthy sisal rug, floral-patterned throw pillows, and hot pink and blue fabrics are layered to create this springy garden theme.

ABOVE RIGHT A pair of wing chairs goes from stiff to cozy when draped with textural, monochromatic throws and pillows.

LEFT Layer texture into an all-white living room. When draped with fabric, a sofa takes on a luxurious feel; subtly patterned pillows break up the white space.

OPPOSITE PAGE Varying textures enhance the tactile experience of a room. Here, furry throw pillows on a woven grass chair and a burlap-covered pillow on a linen slipcovered couch provide contrast and interest.

Rooms with History

One black accent wall anchors a space with soaring ceilings and emphasizes the depth of the recessed wall. A high row of artwork creates a focal point for the room.

If you live in an old house, you may have the benefit of architectural features like exposed beams, decorative molding, historic windows, and wood- or coal-burning fireplaces. Architectural details add history and warmth, so don't hesitate to show them off.

Fireplaces

A fireplace grounds and adds character to a room. Often the focal point of the space, a fireplace also makes a good display area. If your hearth is in disrepair, give it an easy makeover: Apply a coat or two of glossy white paint to imperfect brick or wood,

and your space will seem larger and lighter. Display pictures, candles, favorite vases, or treasured found objects on the mantel. When not in use, the firebox becomes a place to showcase a spray of seasonal greenery or a potted plant.

Play up your room's other architectural details whenever possible by treating them like indoor sculptures. Show off exposed wood beams, or paint moldings a different color from the walls so they stand out. Repair and freshen beadboard walls and play off their lines with graphic black-and-white photos. Keep historic windows painted, in good repair, and, whenever possible, bare.

ABOVE LEFT In a mostly monochromatic room, exposed beams, textured adobe walls, and subtle patterns provide plenty of texture.

TOP RIGHT If you have a wood-burning fireplace, play up the warmth of the hearth with decorative candles.

BOTTOM RIGHT A mantel display needn't be too formal. Pictures set against the wall make for a dynamic tableau over a vintage hearth.

ABOVE LEFT Fili-greed furnishings set under exposed beams and a vaulted ceiling bring elegant contrast to the room.

ABOVE RIGHT Few furnishings are needed in a room with such sculptural

details as waxed pine floors, a curved corner fireplace, and original moldings.

RIGHT A freshly painted exposed brick wall can be a coveted architectural feature and display area in any room.

OPPOSITE PAGE Wood paneling in this old barn becomes a dramatic backdrop for black-and-white photography and an old farm tool dis-played prominently above the beams.

INTERIOR DESIGNER
TRACEY RAPISARDI ON

Architectural Details

The architecture of your living room will help determine how you design it. Architectural elements give a room lots of texture, so use colors and patterns. For true cottage style, architectural details should be simple and clean. Keep window treatments simple with plantation shutters or linen shades that blend into the space to complement these features.

Collections and Display

Save space on bookshelves for personal mementos. Such treasures will make a naturally integrated display when combined with your books.

Artwork, books, and collections are the soul of a living room. The more personal your collections and displays are, the more of a unique character your room will have. Objects need not be rare or valuable for them to have meaning. If a menu from a memorable meal or an old children's book illustration is dear to you, have it framed and hang it on a wall. "Surround yourself with the things that make you happy and things that you love," suggests designer Paula Smail. "It's not about how much something costs; it's about how much you love it."

ABOVE LEFT When displaying collections, group similar items together—either on a wall, shelf, or table-top—for a more unified look.

TOP RIGHT Fuchsia flowers pop in a display of glass and white pottery.

BOTTOM RIGHT Your collections need not be rare or pricey to have value. Display vacation mementos and other personal objects if they have meaning to you.

LEFT When solidly packed with volumes, bookshelves can feel heavy. Break up the space with sculptural objects like antlers or candlesticks.

BELOW When hanging a collection of pictures on one wall, keep frames the same color but vary their size and shape for subtle visual interest.

Displaying Treasures and Books

For easy-on-the-eye displays, create unified groupings such as black-and-white photographs hung on a wall or a cluster of white and cream-colored pottery on the mantel. Coffee table books piled on a rustic wooden bench beckon visitors to thumb through them. A series of medium-scale vintage mirrors can transform a wall and enlarge the space.

A library—or even a suggestion of one—makes a living room cozy. Be sure to keep your books edited so that you are not stockpiling volumes you no longer use (and thus amassing clutter). For a whimsical display, group books by spine color and create a color-block tableau on your shelves. "Bookshelves are architecture, and architecture helps any space," points out interior designer Austin Harrelson. To break up the shelf spaces, he says, "put disparate elements like paintings and objects together to give it character."

Layer your collections with sculptural or translucent objects set against a grouping of framed artwork.

To add your own personal touch, find whimsical pieces that stop the eye but don't take over the room.

Personal Touches

A sense of the unexpected is always welcome in cottage living rooms. Sometimes a room needs a touch of whimsy to make it come alive, so experiment with ways to add your own personal flair. Interior designer Austin Harrelson used a garden sculpture from 17th-century France in his living room. "I love things with quirky individual character," he says. Look for objects that stop you but don't take over the room, he suggests. "Find a piece that has something a little special about it," he recommends, "a piece with a little bit of soul."

If nothing else, play with your living room accessories to make the space interesting. Fanciful pillows, throws, and rugs in bold colors or graphic patterns give the room personality and can be changed when the mood suits you.

A discarded sign becomes an over-sized piece of art that makes this living space unique.

INTERIOR DESIGNERS
ALISHA PETERSON AND
SUSAN DELURGIO ON

Playing with Scale

We like to use scale to add personality and trick the eye. One huge mirror or piece of artwork can make the room. Even in a small space, one oversized piece can give a room that open feeling people crave.

OPPOSITE PAGE, TOP LEFT One blown-up black-and-white photograph solidifies the graphic look of this clean-lined room.

OPPOSITE PAGE, TOP RIGHT A tiny silver spoon—perhaps a memento from a baby's first year—is an unexpected addition to a grouping of framed art.

OPPOSITE PAGE, BOTTOM LEFT Spikey coral is a playful contrast to a geometric photo display.

OPPOSITE PAGE, BOTTOM RIGHT A tiered display of fanciful objects encourages the eye to move around the room.

RIGHT Playful touches, such as an antique toy train, pieces of folk art, or an old wooden ladder, lighten the mood and let visitors know they can relax.

Bringing the Outdoors In

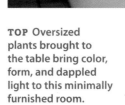

ABOVE This seating area has the fresh feel of an enchanted garden. The piano and chandelier add an unexpected elegance.

OPPOSITE PAGE Multiple plants hung from the ceiling give the impression of being under a canopy of trees in a room with wicker furniture built for outdoor use.

Natural elements and a connection to the outdoors breathe life into living rooms. To bring this freshness indoors, "create an invitation outside," landscape designer Molly Wood advises. If you have windows looking onto a garden, create a focal point for the view like a sculpture or birdbath, she suggests. Wood also recommends bringing a large outdoor plant inside to create a garden-like ambience. "Using an exterior application inside is not a big commitment," she points out. "You can take a plant inside for a month, then cycle it in and out as needed."

Garden Furnishings

Using garden furniture inside also lightens a room, as many designers on our panel point out. A metal garden table and chairs or a piece or two of wicker (paint it black for added elegance) or rattan freshens and adds texture. To tie the room to the seasons, gather flowers, fruit, and greenery from your garden or farmers market and display them in large sculptural vases or bowls. Bring in beautiful objects found in nature—shells, rocks, or branches—to give the space an organic feel.

TOP Oversized plants brought to the table bring color, form, and dappled light to this minimally furnished room.

BOTTOM Multiples of the same plant reinforce the graphic repetition of the windows and beams.

Use a combination of
large and small plants
set at different heights
to create the lush feel
of an indoor garden.

In a room with a garden view, group seating areas around the windows and use plenty of natural materials to play up the garden theme.

Chapter 4

Bedrooms

What has happened to our beloved bedrooms? Thanks to 24/7 technology, they seem to have morphed into media rooms and work-stations. Cottage bedrooms turn down the noise. They are meant chiefly for sleeping and relaxing so you can recharge for the next day. They are quiet, tactile spaces, not multitasking hubs. So give yourself a much needed rest from all the stimulation and information out there. Banish the television. Let your feet fall on a soft cotton rug and your body be enveloped by fresh, crisp sheets. Open the window or a good book, and be sure to turn off your phone.

Combining several textile patterns using similar or harmonious colors creates a homey and welcoming bed.

Slumber in Serenity

A collection of vintage wood was crafted into a sculptural art piece above a simple slip-covered head-board. Linen bedding emphasizes the beachy feel.

Once you begin to prioritize a good night's rest, cottage style comes naturally in the bedroom. Furnish the space with things that are warm and soft to the touch. Use wooden furnishings and all-natural fabrics. Layer the space with soft rugs on the floor and cozy blankets on the bed. Keep the space uncluttered.

The focus of a bedroom is generally the bed itself. It's a good idea to buy the best one you can afford, but furniture in a cottage room needn't be fancy. Look for simple rather than ornate styles. A country or "Swedish" bed, with a wooden headboard and footboard, looks casual and exudes warmth. Victorian wrought-iron beds boast an appealing hand-forged quality. (Note that vintage wrought-iron beds may not comform to standard mattress sizes, so a reproduction may be a better bet.) Low-to-the-ground platform beds also fit the bill. Or, for an unfettered feel, use a simple bed frame and improvise a whimsical headboard fashioned from a vintage folding screen or favorite quilt. What you put on the bed is just as important as the frame. If you are in the market for a new mattress, opt for an organic one to keep toxins out of your bedroom.

ABOVE Keep distractions like TVs to a minimum. Carve out a comfortable reading nook by a window. In a predominantly white room, look for contrasting textures to add visual interest.

LEFT The curved headboard of this painted wooden bedframe features a scrollwork pattern that complements the ruffled white sheets and floral bedspread.

A Layered Bed

How to best dress a bed for cottage style? Layer it with crisp sheets and soft, tactile blankets in natural materials like wool, mohair, or angora. "Layers provide warmth and comfort," designer Paula Smail points out. Smail encourages mixing different fabrics on the bed for added comfort and visual interest. "Blending silk, cotton, and velvet all together provides beautiful contrast and texture," she says.

For a minimalist style, choose a fitted sheet in white or ivory paired with a white duvet, matching pillowcases, and two throw pillows for a jolt of color. The linens need not match. Choose floral-patterned pillowcases to complement solid sheets; a neutral top sheet can accompany any fitted sheets. Avoid an overly fussy bed piled with bolsters and shams, as the effect will be busy, not calming. Standard pillows (you may want to double up for maximum comfort while reading in bed) with a throw pillow or two on top create a simple but finished look. Freshen the look of your bed with the seasons. Cool, crisp cotton or linen breathes well in summer, while flannel is a nice option in the cooler months.

A linen bedspread and gray striped sheets allow the art collection to take center stage. To mimic this design, take illustrated pages from an old book, then frame and hang them together in a unified fashion.

INTERIOR DESIGNERS ALISHA PETERSON
AND SUSAN DELURGIO ON

The Elements of a Cottage Bedroom

Keep the bedroom simple with a painted bed, a dresser and nightstand, and as little other furniture as possible. Linens and blankets should be soft and cozy. We love vintage blankets in white hues that have a softness you can't buy. Creamy white walls are a bedroom must (the space will automatically feel twice as big), combined with a pop of color, which could come from a quilt, painted headboard, or happy piece of wall art.

ABOVE The same hues of pink are featured in the wallpaper and quilt, creating a cohesive look even though the patterns do not match.

LEFT This clean white bed is layered to perfection with a wool comforter, cotton blanket and sheets, and extra pillows for reading.

Furniture

Most likely your bed will help define the room's layout and overall tone. Once you have established a sleep "zone," carve out other areas for dressing and relaxing. If you have the space, create an intimate seating area, preferably by the window, for reading. Define the space with a small sofa or deep-seated armchair and a place to put down a book or coffee cup.

Improvisation is welcome in a cottage bedroom, so have fun with alternative-style nightstands. If you are in the habit of storing books and personal items bedside, a small wooden cabinet or chest painted white can suit almost any room. An imaginative alternative, such as an old writing desk, wooden file cabinet, or stacks of handsome vintage suitcases, will give the room personality and a touch of the unexpected.

Storage

Freestanding wooden armoires, dressers, and chests provide extra storage and infuse a bedroom with warmth. If possible, use pieces that have a history, such as something handed down from a relative or plucked from a garage sale. Freshen a stained or chipped piece with a coat of creamy white or ivory paint.

Lighting

Choose colors, textures, and lighting that feel soothing and calm. Lighting should be adjustable, with a combination of overhead and task lights. Table lamps or sconces allow you to customize light for reading. Go for serene rather than stimulating hues on the walls. Neutrals feel relaxing; cool colors like blue, violet, and gray are soothing.

OPPOSITE PAGE A slipcovered headboard and a painted white nightstand are pieces that can last a lifetime.

TOP Dress up hand-me-down bureaus with a new coat of paint. A chair with a washable slipcover is a practical choice in a cottage bedroom.

BOTTOM A vintage armoire and settee provide period charm to a brick-walled bedroom. Armoires are the perfect solution to limited closet space.

ABOVE LEFT This headboard also serves as a nightstand, bookshelf, and surface for reading lights.

LEFT If your bedroom has natural light, add a plant for texture and cleaner indoor air. The dresser in this room gives the space a sense of history.

ABOVE RIGHT A round end table makes the most of tight corner space.

OPPOSITE PAGE Matching lamps on the nightstands provide ambient and reading light. The upholstered headboard and skirt provide a punch of color and can be changed to freshen the room's decor.

Floors and Windows

Wood floors give a bedroom a sense of history and warmth. Soften hardwood floors (and layer carpeted floors) with tactile area and throw rugs. Place two small flokati rugs, dhurries, or sheepskins by each bed to help warm cold morning feet. Keep window treatments simple with curtains light enough to billow in a breeze or with informal shades. Avoid heavy draperies that will weigh down the room. "We often use white cotton curtain panels that give privacy but still let the sunshine filter in," point out interior designers Susan Delurgio and Alisha Peterson. Café-style curtains and shades that come down from the middle of the window also allow for privacy and light. Bamboo shades add an appealing textural element.

The more you personalize your bedroom, the more comfortable it will feel, as long as you don't let the space get cluttered. Family photos, whimsical artwork, and favorite books are reassuring reminders of who we are and where we've been.

RIGHT Layer wood floors with soft area rugs. A combination of overhead and task lighting is ideal in the bedroom.

OPPOSITE PAGE, TOP Large French doors provide abundant natural light in this room with painted white floors and blue accents.

OPPOSITE PAGE, BOTTOM LEFT Narrow-strip plank floors are given new life with a whitewash stain that brightens the entire room. A small rug keeps feet warm until you can find your slippers.

OPPOSITE PAGE, BOTTOM RIGHT High windows sometimes don't need any coverings, making it possible to save energy by avoiding the use of electric lighting throughout the day.

Small-Space Bedrooms

For a more expansive feel, keep walls and floors white in a small bedroom. Use pops of colorful accessories to enliven the space.

In older houses especially, sleeping quarters sometimes exist in small or oddly shaped rooms. Sometimes the smaller the bedroom, the cozier it feels, but there are ways to make the space seem more open. Walls and furnishings painted white or a neutral color will make them appear to recede and make your room look bigger, as can a large mirror hung or propped against a wall.

This can be especially useful in an attic or dormer bedroom. Bring in a small table or desk and a comfortable chair so that the room doesn't get swallowed up by the bed. Bolder wall hues may contain the space and make it feel more intimate. If you like the feel of being cocooned, surround the room with books, artwork, or wallpaper for a library-like setting.

ABOVE LEFT To emphasize the intimacy of a small bedroom, surround the space with books and art.

TOP RIGHT Built-in cabinets make the most of an awkwardly shaped wall. Metal trash containers blend in with the painted iron bed frame and provide more closed storage.

BOTTOM RIGHT In a guest room that doubles as a home office, keep a small footprint for the bed by adding a trundle underneath a twin and you'll still be able to accommodate two people.

Guest Rooms

Make guest room furnishings versatile. A small writing desk doubles as a nightstand, while a slipper chair at the end of the bed provides seating and a place for clothes.

Guest rooms should have a special feel all their own. If you have a flair for hospitality, this is the place to show it. Any guest space can sparkle with touches like fresh flowers, a scented candle, reading materials, and glass bottles of mineral water.

A room for guests needs to be private and, if it is a dual-function space, versatile. "Guest room furnishings should be cozy, comfortable, and washable," notes interior designer Tracey Rapisardi, who favors slipcovered pieces for practical guest spaces. "Guest rooms should not be too formal; they should be fun. Use furnishings people can really live with."

Many guest rooms double as an office or playroom. In these cases, furnishings should be selected carefully to allow for flexibility and smart storage. Versatile pieces are a must. Choose a bed that can be used for seating during the day, such as an iron daybed or trundle bed.

Have a mattress cover made so that you can style the bed like a couch. Baskets and trunks can provide seasonal storage for you and be used as end tables for visitors. If the room is big enough, Rapisardi suggests, a place to sit is always appreciated, so your guest is not always confined to the bed.

RIGHT Depending on which guests visit most, twin beds may be a practical option for a spare room. In a small guest room, matching beds and nightstands unify the space. Fresh flowers welcome incoming visitors.

BELOW Flexible storage is essential in guest rooms. A freestanding armoire can hide office supplies or toys and accommodate guests' clothes.

INTERIOR DESIGNERS ALISHA
PETERSON AND SUSAN DELURGIO ON

Welcoming Guests

Guest rooms should make visitors feel at home. Provide them with a sweet cottage dresser for their belongings and a cheery nightstand complete with garden flowers. It's also fun to leave a homemade guest book out for friends and family to write you notes about their visits.

Storage

Guest rooms should function as year-round storage for you, but overnight visitors feel more welcome when there is space for their belongings as well. Designate some closet space to visitors, or use a freestanding armoire with a hanging rack on one side and storage space for office supplies or toys on the other. Provide extra hangers and towels and, if possible, a place to store luggage. In a weekend or vacation cottage, where frequent guests may be the norm, it's nice to include extra toiletries like shampoo and toothpaste in personalized wire tote baskets.

In a room that is used only for guests, you can go all out with a full-size bed or two twin beds. Equip the room with a dresser and mirror and place a bench for luggage and seating at the end of the bed. Keep the space uncluttered, and resist the urge to house a television there. Visitors come to relax and spend time with you, not catch up on world events.

ABOVE Vintage iron beds provide endless charm in a guest room but may require custom mattresses, as they were manufactured before sizes were standardized.

LEFT Personalized touches like casually displayed artwork keep a guest room from feeling like a hotel.

OPPOSITE PAGE Niceties like hand towels and fresh flowers by the bed make guests feel more welcome.

Kids' Rooms

In children's bedrooms, wall colors will have longevity if you keep them neutral. Carve out one or two areas for whimsy, such as a wallpapered ceiling or accent wall.

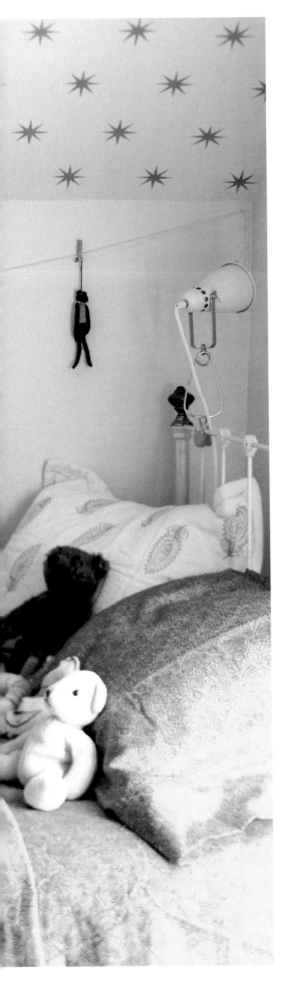

Shelves are a must in a child's room. Bookcases or floating wall shelves accommodate not only books but also baskets of toys and supplies and even an artwork display.

Cottage style is especially well-suited to children' rooms, which need to be hard-wearing, versatile spaces kids can grow into. A simple or secondhand wooden dresser, desk, and bookshelf will suit many children's needs, especially when freshly painted and outfitted with personalized knobs or drawer pulls. A vintage school desk, trunk, or bench adds charm. Trundle beds, bunk beds, or two twin beds provide space for sleepovers or visiting cousins.

If space allows, provide a comfortable old armchair or sofa in a slipcovered washable fabric so your child can curl up and read. Keep walls neutral but allow your child to personalize the space with wallpaper, paint, or decals on an accent wall. Adorn the space with your child's artwork in basic wooden frames and replace them with updated pieces as your child matures. Provide lots of woven baskets, painted metal buckets and wooden bins or cubbies for corralling toys and sports equipment.

ABOVE LEFT A wooden dresser painted white is ideal for children's rooms. It can be customized with knobs and drawer pulls or repainted down the road.

LEFT A wooden trouser hanger hung from a basic hook is a clever method for a changing artwork or calendar display above the desk.

ABOVE RIGHT Casual cottage-style bedrooms are ideal for whimsical play areas, such as this fort made of old curtain panels. A vintage child's rocking chair painted bright blue provides a burst of color.

OPPOSITE PAGE Avoid making kids' rooms too theme-oriented, as children are likely to outgrow the space quickly. Keep the space neutral and flexible and let kids customize one wall with favorite art or toy displays.

Chapter 5

Bathrooms

Cottage-style bathrooms reflect the simplicity of an earlier time, when the bathroom was a purely utilitarian space stripped to its basic elements. Imagine Kohler's first indoor bathtub, an enameled cast-iron claw-footed affair advertised in 1883 as a "horse trough/ hog scalder, when furnished with four legs will serve as a bathtub."

Sculptural and elegant, claw-foot tubs were the norm in the early 20th century but became outmoded with later models. Today the nostalgia of the vintage tub and the romance it evokes are at the heart of cottage-style bathrooms.

Wainscoting, an antique claw-foot tub, and a pedestal sink are the three pillars of a cottage-style bathroom.

Good Clean Design

In a juxtaposition of styles, worn wood flooring, period fixtures, and white wainscot are combined with a modern double vanity.

In the early days, bathing was a luxury. It took time. In many homes, bathing was relegated to a Saturday night, when there was time to heat enough water for the whole family, and everyone went to bed cleaned up and ready for church the next day.

In our age of efficiency, of quick showers and fast-acting cleansers, the notion of soaking leisurely in a beautiful bathtub on a Saturday night seems almost decadent. Of course, it is precisely that feeling we long for, when a warm bath was an evening's event.

Thanks to modern conveniences, today we can expect a truly luxurious bathing experience with plentiful hot water, milled soaps, thick towels, and central heating. In many cottages, the bathroom is a welcome refuge after a day at the beach or exploring outdoors. After all, there is nothing more rewarding than a hot shower after a day's adventure. With the right approach, you can easily put the pleasure back into bathing and grooming. Plentiful light, tactile accessories, and attractive storage can turn a blah bathroom into an oasis of comfort and style.

Architectural Details

Early American houses were constructed simply with a plethora of wood.

A typical 100-year-old cottage might have been paneled with beadboard or wainscoting. Sculptural fixtures were freestanding. Hand-forged hardware was of the sturdy, heavy variety. These details make a bathroom feel comfortable and solid, so if you are fortunate enough to have such features in your bathroom, make the most of them.

TOP LEFT Make the most of natural light and views in the bathroom. This custom tub is well-positioned for a sun-splashed soak.

TOP RIGHT In a bathroom, hooks can be more versatile than standard towel racks for storing multiple towels and robes.

BOTTOM RIGHT Sea blue shower tiles offset the room's streamlined fixtures. Cool hues have a calming effect on bathers.

DESIGNER
PAULA SMAIL ON

Bathroom Do's and Don'ts

Follow these tips to create a warm and welcoming bathroom.

DO: Keep things organized. Hang art on the walls. Add scented soaps and candles and fresh flowers. Add a chair or a dresser if you have the space.

DON'T: Overwhelm a small bathroom with too much fabric in window treatments and shower curtains. Be so minimal that it is sterile. Have so much stuff on the counter that it stops being a fun place to hang out.

Bathroom Basics

Bathrooms need not have original fixtures to feel inviting. Fixture styles abound. If you are choosing new ones, let the layout of your room and your own tastes guide you. Freestanding pieces lend charm, though built-in fixtures can be more practical, particularly when storage is tight. Master baths sometimes call for an extra touch of luxury, such as a deep soaking tub or an antique armoire, while hard-wearing kids' bathrooms need durable flooring and cabinets. Whatever style you choose, let simplicity and clean lines dictate your decision.

TOP RIGHT Don't hesitate to adorn a bathroom with a favorite piece of artwork, as long as it's not a rare masterpiece.

BOTTOM RIGHT Wall-mounted faucets have a sleek, streamlined look. Contrast stone's coolness with textural objects like fluffy towels and woven baskets.

Wall Finishes

A fresh coat of paint keeps the bathroom looking clean and inviting. Neutral colors make bathrooms relaxing, but go for bold hues if you like them. Use a VOC-free paint in an eggshell or semigloss finish. If you have paneling, stain it a wood tone or paint it white. Wallpaper isn't the best option for bathroom walls, as moisture can get trapped behind the surface or make the paper peel. Use wallpaper sparingly in half baths or separate water closets.

Glass tiles extend high enough on the wall to provide recessed storage around the soaking tub. Sky blue paint continues the calming trend.

Large porcelain tiles are sturdy and easy to keep clean, making them an especially good choice for bathrooms with an exterior entry door.

Flooring Options

Basic porcelain floor tiles in small hexagons or squares give the room an established look and are easy to keep clean. Use rugs to add warmth and prevent slips. Some older houses feature softwood flooring in the bathroom, which gives the space a homey feel. Historically, such floors were often painted to dress up the wood. Consider painting your less-than-perfect wood all one color or a period-style checkerboard design. Use paint designed for use on the floor, and apply two coats of clear, low-VOC polyurethane sealant for added protection. Wood floors should be kept as dry as possible and are not the best option for a hard-wearing bathroom.

Guest Bathrooms

There are special considerations for guest and half bathrooms. Keep both clean and uncluttered. Stock them with towels, soaps, shampoos, and toilet tissue for visitors' convenience. Provide linen or cotton hand towels next to the sink; fanciful dish towels can add a touch of whimsy. If space allows, install extra hooks and carve out storage space in the guest bath. Infuse the room with fragrance by using subtle candles or, when possible, fresh flowers.

LEFT Painted wood flooring adds cottage style to a bathroom, and paint helps protect the wood from water, but such floors will fare better in less frequently used baths and half baths.

RIGHT Guests will appreciate having their own shelf in the bathroom, with baskets to keep things separated and stacks of fresh towels.

Vintage-Style Baths

A 1930s bath is restored to its original beauty.

Vintage furnishings feel right at home in the cottage bathroom. A claw-foot tub, pedestal sink, or antique tiles will provide period charm. Extend the look with a vintage armoire for storing towels, lovely old mirrors, and generous storage baskets to infuse even more warmth. If you are new to a house with original vintage fixtures, consider keeping them in place and working around them, even if they look worn, suggests interior designer Tracey Rapisardi. If the tub or sink is chipped or rusted, it can be resurfaced, Rapisardi points out.

"Especially in newly built homes, a vintage tub or sink gives the bathroom a cottage feel," notes interior designer Alisha Peterson. You can find these items at online retailers or salvage yards around the country. If the idea of using a 100-year-old bathtub doesn't suit you but you like vintage style, choose a reproduction fixture. Both pedestal sinks (traditional and modern versions) and wash-basin-style sinks (flat top, typically marble, with visible plumbing) are attractive choices, as are console sinks. The one drawback to these sink styles is a lack of storage.

In the Details

Sometimes just a hint of vintage is enough. Consider installing antique or reproduction faucets, hardware, or door-knobs for an old-world feel. Whatever style you choose, keep it consistent, or compatible, with the room's towel bars, shower rods, and hooks. Stainless-steel, chrome, and nickel finishes are good choices for both vintage and contemporary bathrooms. Antique wooden medicine cabinets and period sconces also give a space a sense of history. New versions of old-style wooden medicine cabinets are available through retailers like Pottery Barn and other home stores.

TOP Hexagonal floor tiles paired with white paneling and a painted wooden vanity make this bathroom look like it might have a hundred years ago.

ABOVE Faucets are the bathroom's jewelry. Choose fanciful designs such as this reproduction antique French faucet to make your bathroom shine.

RIGHT A vintage sink and faucets inject this woodsy bath with old-world charm.

LEFT In an old home, keeping the bathroom design within the same period will create a smooth transition from the living space.

OPPOSITE PAGE, TOP LEFT A round pedestal sink and mosaic tiles are a gorgeous still life.

OPPOSITE PAGE, TOP RIGHT Walls don't have to be perfect in a cottage bathroom. Sometimes all that's needed to freshen worn wood is a coat of white paint.

OPPOSITE PAGE, BOTTOM LEFT In a guest bath, a vintage armoire stocked with extra linens and blankets makes visitors feel welcome.

OPPOSITE PAGE, BOTTOM RIGHT There's nothing else quite like an antique claw-foot tub. Add a shelf to the adjacent wall, a bath caddy that stretches across the tub, or a small side table so that toiletries are close at hand.

Accessorizing the Bath

A light fixture and side table designed for a living space make this bathroom feel more like an extension of the rest of the home.

To avoid a chilly clinical feel in the bathroom, warm the space with tactile accessories and personal touches. The first place to start is with bathroom basics like the shower curtain, rug, and towels. Play with color and pattern here, especially if your overall color scheme is neutral. Have a curtain stitched from pretty vintage fabric or hang whimsical dish towels or textural linen hand towels by the sink. A wood-framed mirror hung above the basin can be much more appealing than a traditional medicine cabinet. As for rugs, "think beyond the bathmat," suggests interior designer Liz Williams. Indoor-outdoor rugs are a great choice for the bathroom, she suggests, as are washable cotton striped rugs.

Because bathroom style is often dictated by practical elements, a sense of the unexpected is welcome. Consider outfitting the room with things you might otherwise use in your living room or bedroom, such as a chair, stool, small table, dresser, or armoire. "A bathroom should have a piece of furniture to be interesting," says interior designer Austin Harrelson. Furnishings with texture and warmth make the room especially inviting. A wood-framed mirror, artwork on the walls, and houseplants inject personality.

DESIGNER
PAULA SMAIL ON

Art

Artwork is a great way to add color, interest, and whimsy to the bath. Of course this is not the room to hang an original Matisse if you are lucky enough own one, but there is plenty of affordable art that would look fantastic in the bathroom. I often suggest framed posters, prints, and kids' drawings for this space.

TOP A collection of vintage glass bottles and an early-1900s Red Cross wall cabinet continue the theme set by a rusted claw-foot that has been resurfaced inside.

BOTTOM LEFT The more you personalize a bathroom with touches like candles and plants, the more inviting it becomes.

BOTTOM RIGHT A bench is a versatile choice for both storage and seating.

INTERIOR DESIGNERS
ALISHA PETERSON AND
SUSAN DELURGIO ON

Natural Bathroom Accessories

To play up the natural feel of a cottage bath, we like using objects found in nature to add texture and warmth to an otherwise streamlined space. We'll use pebbles or rocks in the shower and reclaimed-wood frames for mirrors.

Scent and Ambience

An inviting bathroom looks and feels comfortable, and smells nice too. Fragrance in small doses is a welcome addition to the bath. Display beautifully packaged candles, perfumes, or soaps on a tray atop a vanity or dresser; their subtle scents will infuse the room. Fresh or dried flowers (such as lavender) can also scent the room while adding color and visual pop. A small bowl of lemons in summer or pomegranates in winter freshens the space and can be left to dry.

Lighting is another way to personalize the bathroom. By day, natural light is ideal. Consider putting ceiling lights on a dimmer switch for softer light while you're soaking in the tub. Decorative sconces by the mirror dress up the space and, if on a dimmer switch, can be adjusted for shaving or makeup application.

ABOVE LEFT Stacked in descending size, lidded baskets, vintage luggage, or linen boxes provide texture and storage.

ABOVE RIGHT A singular piece of furniture, such as this Indian stool with scroll arms, can transform a straightforward bathroom into an inviting space.

OPPOSITE PAGE Fresh flowers and rustic wood accessories give this bath a natural look and feel.

Storage

Quirky cabinets with small drawers are perfect for storing makeup, toiletries, or jewelry.

Bathroom storage needs will vary depending on who is using the room and whether you prefer open or closed storage. Ideally, shelves and drawers in built-in vanities will meet your storage needs, but often more room is required. If you have the space for it, a glass-fronted cabinet or even your grandmother's chest of drawers can provide space to stash makeup and toiletries. Vintage luggage and lidded baskets tucked under the sink provide deep storage while adding texture to the space.

Storage on Display

Open storage, when well organized and maintained, adds visual interest to the room. Sparkling perfume bottles, stacks of fresh towels, and even toilet paper rolls are pleasing to look at when nicely arranged on a shelf. Smaller items can be tucked in woven baskets or translucent containers. House these containers in multiples on a mobile cart or open shelf for maximum effect. Storage vessels should be similarly attractive. Those made of wood, glass, or woven materials contribute to the organic feel of a cottage bath.

ABOVE LEFT Opt for storage pieces made of natural materials like wood instead of plastic. A collection of Turkish towels warrants a pretty display.

ABOVE RIGHT Try displaying soaps in a beautiful glass vessel rather than hiding them in a cabinet.

RIGHT A vintage wire basket and cups made of milk glass keep small bathroom toiletries neat and organized.

Garden Baths

If you have the luxury of a bathroom framed by nature, make the most of it. An old back porch or sunroom that faces the garden can become a lovely bathroom. Generous windows highlight views and can create the feeling of an outdoor room. Where privacy is a concern, consider a simple translucent window treatment like frosted glass, semi-sheer curtains, or solar shades. Bamboo or other woven shades add earthiness.

For a lush atmosphere, bring the outdoors in. Landscape designer Molly Wood suggests using outdoor plants in the bathroom in large textural urns. If you have enough ceiling height, a small tree contributes to the garden setting. Herb topiaries, ferns, and orchids in decorative planters are also beautiful and thrive in moist conditions. Natural materials will highlight the garden aspect of your bathroom. Consider a garden stool or a small wooden bench for a stall shower. Stone flooring, wooden shelves, and linen towels will emphasize the theme, as will groups of woven baskets.

OPPOSITE PAGE Freestanding bathtubs are generally deeper than standard built-ins, and separate faucets mean more room to navigate.

TOP RIGHT A deep soaking tub is perfectly positioned to take in views from the garden.

BOTTOM RIGHT Potted plants or fresh cut flowers bring the beauty of nature to your bathroom and add vibrant color.

O utdoor showers are particularly useful for rinsing off after a day at the beach, and they make for luxurious outdoor bathing in the summer. Choose weather-resistant materials that will stand up to the elements, such as pressure-treated wood, stone, or metal. If you don't want to build your own or hire a professional, portable solar outdoor showers may be a good option. Such models tend to be sleek and modern, but you can soften the design with pretty (and mold-resistant) shower curtains and a decorative planter filled with fresh towels. Be sure to use environmentally friendly soaps and shampoos when bathing outdoors, as harsh chemicals in the water runoff can kill surrounding plants.

ABOVE LEFT Built around an outdoor spigot, this shower includes a raised wooden platform with spaces between the slats so water will drain through the sand-laid brick below.

ABOVE RIGHT If you can't tap into existing plumbing inside the house, buy a ready-made shower that hooks up to a long garden hose.

OPPOSITE PAGE Solid wooden walls provide complete privacy and help keep the space warmer. A series of hooks, a shower caddy, and a built-in bench hold towels and toiletries. Used bathing suits can be set in the hanging wire basket.

Chapter 6

Storage

Here's a secret about storage: It needn't be a chore. Cottage-style storage means thinking—literally—outside the cardboard box and finding panache in what you stash. Storage options have never been more appealing and abundant, so it's easy to choose beautiful, workable solutions. Turn your storage needs into a subtle style statement. Find pretty baskets for magazines or laundry, use an old wine crate to organize table linens, or turn a library card catalog from the flea market into a handsome cabinet for recipes or craft supplies.

Make storage stylish. Lidded baskets and neatly stacked magazines add texture and form to the "dead space" under a console.

Streamlined Storage

Cottage style eschews clutter, so invest some time in organizing and storing your belongings. Design experts on our panel agree that effective storage solutions begin with smart editing. Take an inventory of what you have and do a good purge before you organize what goes where. Store only things you absolutely need.

Recycle or pass on items you don't use at least once a year. Then decide what should be kept close at hand for everyday use and what can go into deep storage. Finally, a label maker will help you keep tabs on your things.

Set Good Habits

Everyday items are often the hardest to corral. A place for keys, mail, toys, and gadgets is essential. Keep baskets in your entryway for discarded items and establish a central mail station. If you have small children, use rolling bins or pretty fabric carts to gather up toys and store them out of sight when needed.

Multiuse storage is especially effective. A storage unit under a window can also function as a window seat with the right cushions.

Ottomans with storage capacity inside are useful in bathrooms, living rooms, and bedrooms.

Other storage options generally fall into open or hidden categories. Try to fit your belongings into one of these groups, keeping aesthetics in mind. Books add texture and interest to a room, while file folders don't. A small vintage cabinet might be a great choice for storing extra toiletries in the bathroom. Glass jars in the kitchen show off beans and legumes and provide a homey, rustic feel. Whenever possible, choose containers made of natural materials like wood, glass, or fabric. Banish plastic if you can.

ABOVE Create a uniform look by storing items in matching baskets on shelves. Hanging tags quickly tell you what's in them.

LEFT The more attractive your storage, the more likely you are to maintain it. Use a sculptural vessel to hold mail or other small items.

OPPOSITE PAGE Keeping items neatly folded, stacked, and arranged is one of the keys to successful and attractive storage.

Open Storage

Shelves are probably the most ubiquitous and flexible form of storage because they can be configured in countless ways.

Shelves can go in any room and with any color scheme. Wooden shelves feel classic and warm, while metal versions signal contemporary style. Built-in shelves feel more integrated into the room, while freestanding cases complement a room like furniture. Refurbish worn-wood shelves with a creamy coat of paint.

The Power of Multiples

Shelves are also a terrific organizing method for smaller containers like square baskets, magazine binders, and decorative boxes. Using multiples of any one option will result in a cohesive, streamlined look that keeps clutter to a minimum.

Hooks

Never underestimate the power of hooks. Placed singly, staggered, or in a row, hooks are a great catchall for coats, dish towels, bathrobes, reusable grocery shopping bags, and more. The bathroom, pantry, entryway, and closet can all benefit from hooks.

ABOVE Open storage requires an organizing method to keep it clutter-free. The serving pieces displayed on this hutch are grouped by color, shape, and size.

LEFT Create a "coat rack" in the kitchen for beautiful cloth napkins, dish towels, and aprons.

OPPOSITE PAGE Bookcases aren't just for your favorite volumes. They are also a great space for magazine binders, table linens, and other items that can be grouped by type.

LANDSCAPE DESIGNER
MOLLY WOOD ON

Clear Storage Containers

I like to store items in clear containers as often as possible. For example, I have several lidded Lucite boxes in my bathroom; one is full of bars of soap, another cotton swabs, and so on. The visual reminder that you are fully stocked with these items feels both decadent and functional.

LEFT Use hidden spaces for extra shelving. Here, four carefully placed shelves turn the space underneath a staircase into a nifty home office.

OPPOSITE PAGE Paint the wall behind an open shelving system for a punch of color in an otherwise monochromatic display.

Closed Storage

Closed storage solutions keep things organized and out of sight. Chests, cupboards and armoires offer a discreet place to stash anything from guest towels to extra batteries. Keep the scale on a human level, as deep, hulking armoires can take over a room. Vintage versions supply character and a good hiding place.

To maximize hidden storage, blogger Mina Brinkey suggests finding "dead spaces" such as the area under the bed or in the upper reaches of your closet to store blankets, off-season clothes, or other things you don't need regularly. Use attractive boxes or zippered bags and label each accordingly.

ABOVE Look for one-of-a-kind cabinets such as this antique library card catalog (used for recipes) at flea markets or tag sales.

LEFT A distinctive cabinet can add instant character to any room, especially when styled attractively.

OPPOSITE PAGE Just because they are hidden, under-the-bed storage containers needn't be unsightly. Find attractive solutions that work with your decor and organize them appropriately.

Decorative Storage

Old wooden crates are a charming and environmentally friendly alternative to plastic.

ABOVE Rolling carts are ideal for corralling toys, ferrying laundry, or stashing extra towels.

TOP RIGHT Brightly hued baskets add instant color to any space; change them out for another option when the mood strikes.

BOTTOM RIGHT Keep summer sandals in woven baskets for a grab-and-go solution when heading to the beach.

Decorative storage containers can add just the right pop of color or texture to a room. Think of decorative storage pieces as accessories. Choose textural baskets for magazines, throw pillows, and laundry. Find a sculptural vessel for incoming mail. Silver or aluminum buckets can hold extra towels or silverware. Stacks of tiny boxes keep jewelry easily accessible while adding panache to the top of your dresser.

INTERIOR DESIGNER
TRACEY RAPISARDI ON

Cottage Storage

Older houses weren't built with a lot of storage, so we've come to use accessories to stow things. I like pieces with character, such as an old bureau or chest. Some of my favorite options for storing smaller items are vintage or salvaged and have lots of old charm: glass jars, wire baskets, old canisters, and even old breadboxes. You just have to have fun with it.

When thoughtfully grouped, books and magazines add color and graphic interest to a room. Display them both vertically and horizontally to break up the space.

A ladder-style wooden magazine rack lets you keep track of—and cull—your publications more easily.

Chapter 7

Palettes

Cottage colors aren't announced abruptly. They are subtle hues that reveal themselves slowly over time. A room that appears milk white during the day may shift to an earthy taupe as the sun dips and lamps within the room are lit. Like the natural landscape from which it is derived, the cottage palette is restrained, even elusive, always changing. The stunning result is color that expands the room and calms the mind.

Even subtle color can transform a space. Be sure to test a range of hues in varying light before you paint a room.

Color Considerations

Paint an accent wall a deeper shade than the rest of the room for added definition and drama.

Our eyes see color in many different ways: in relation to light, in contrast with other hues, and in textural relief. A white brick wall will look different from a glossy white wood floor when light and shadow come into play. The subtlety of soft color is what makes cottage palettes shine.

Subtle Shades

To create spaces that look open and feel calm, look for lighter colors in neutral or natural tones. Select hues that don't compete with the shapes and textures of the room. Cottage rooms feel cozy and tactile, so use neutral colors to emphasize these qualities. Off-white walls will set off dark-wood furniture to a dramatic effect. A room bathed in café au lait will ground a space filled with white wicker furnishings.

Colors that are so subtle they are hard to name are often the most intriguing. "I love ethereal colors that you can't put your finger on," says interior designer Austin Harrelson, who favors soft, subdued shades. "Sometimes when the light hits it, you never know what you are going to get."

When selecting colors, note the distinction between warm hues and cool ones. Warm colors such as yellow, red, and brown have a stimulating effect and can make a room seem smaller or more intimate. Cool shades—blues, greens, some grays—have a calming effect and can make a room feel more expansive. Note that even colors that appear off-white contain some color pigment and generally fall into warm or cool categories.

Remember to test several colors at different times of the day and in different light before you choose one. And know that paint is far from permanent, so when you grow tired of one color, it's easy to change it.

Textural materials in your room—a wood floor or linen curtains—become even more tactile in neutral shades.

INTERIOR DESIGNER
TRACEY RAPISARDI ON

Painted Floors

Painted floors evoke true cottage style. Back in the early days, cottage floors were generally made of pine, a softwood that wears heavily, and were often painted to hide years of damage. When working with softwood floors, consider painting them to freshen the room and add a finished look. You can paint them white or tint them with a soft apple green or sea glass. Painted floors finish off the bones of the room and work especially well in bedrooms and kitchens.

Neutrals

To emphasize subtle color variations, think about ways to incorporate texture in your living space. Here, linen, wood, cowhide, stone, and brick create an inviting palette all their own.

Cottage rooms are quiet, and a neutral palette helps maintain that sense of calm. Soft whites, grays, taupe, and cream are subtle enough to play up a room's textures without overpowering it. Neutrals set off texture, notes landscape designer Molly Wood. "Materials like sea grass and linen look so rich and earthy next to neutral colors."

Finding Personality

Neutral doesn't have to mean no color, points out interior designer Austin Harrelson. "Neutral means you can mix anything with it," he says. In fact, a world of possibility exists within the neutral palette. "People think white and beige are not colors, but they have distinct personalities," maintains designer Paula Smail.

Depending on how you use them, neutrals can be dramatic, romantic, serene, or crisp. For example, for added visual interest, use a slightly deeper color than that of your walls for the ceiling, suggests interior designer Liz Williams. "This adds drama, especially if you have high ceilings," Williams says.

Patterned pillowcases, a dark-wood nightstand, and a woven basket make a white bedroom feel cozy.

OPPOSITE PAGE, TOP LEFT A pale bluish-white paint on the top half of the wall subtly emphasizes the shape of this room.

OPPOSITE PAGE, TOP RIGHT Varying degrees of natural and incandescent light can dramatically change wall color. A painted accent wall may go from subtle to serious depending on illumination.

OPPOSITE PAGE, BOTTOM LEFT Textural elements create shadow and depth, making neutral colors come alive.

OPPOSITE PAGE, BOTTOM RIGHT Natural materials like stone and wood add visual interest in an all-white space.

ABOVE Shades of white take on distinct character when juxtaposed together or with an earthy dark brown.

Inspired by Nature

<table>
</table>

Many of the designers on our panel are most at home with colors inspired by nature. "The color in your house will depend on where you are— on the coastline, in the mountains. Your colors should reflect the environment," says interior designer Tracey Rapisardi. If your cottage has a view of the ocean, you may want to echo those hues indoors. A house in the woods might take on an earthy palette, while one in an open meadow may include soft greens with bursts of wildflower color.

"In rooms with lots of windows, the colors should be chosen taking your landscape colors into consideration," notes Austin Harrelson.

ABOVE Use your landscape to inspire color choices indoors. Here, blue has a calming effect, evoking the sky and sea.

TOP RIGHT In a room with a view, look to the natural elements outdoors to inspire the palette inside.

BOTTOM RIGHT Bring one accent color in varying shades and textures into a room to enliven the space.

Dark and Light

Dark and light rooms have a strong graphic appeal. Glossy brown paint makes the white ceiling, trim, and furnishings pop.

Black and white or dark brown and gray mixed with white or cream have a strong graphic appeal that can be subtle or dramatic. Dark colors ground a room, while whites expand it, and each will intensify the other when both are used together. You can use black or charcoal gray pillows to anchor a white sofa or paint an accent wall black or chocolate to ground a white room. Note that the color's finish—glossy, matte, or somewhere in between—will affect how the eye reads it. Glossy finishes are more reflective and pick up light easily, giving the surface texture and depth.

ABOVE Blond wood flooring makes a black-and-white kitchen less stark. The back wall is painted with chalkboard paint for kids to draw on while adults cook dinner.

LEFT Having trouble choosing colors? Varying shades of white, black, and gray give a room graphic appeal.

Color Accents

Small amounts of a bold color can make a big statement.

Most designers on our panel agree that accents and accessories are a good way to introduce color into cottage rooms. One painted wall or pile of colorful pillows can give a room depth. "Painted accent walls pull the eye's attention somewhere," designer Paula Smail points out. Don't hesitate to use bold hues when accenting your space. "There is no such thing as right or wrong color,"

Smail says. "It just needs to be a color you like."

Blogger Mina Brinkey likes to use colorful accessories that change with the seasons. "Browns and burnt oranges are good colors for fall," she notes. As for which accessories to choose, Brinkey suggests colorful pottery, chandeliers, rugs, or a painted accent wall.

ABOVE LEFT In a bathroom with white tiled wainscot, a robin's egg blue on the upper walls and ceilings gives the space a sense of refinement.

TOP RIGHT In a neutral room, opt for stronger colors in easily changeable pieces, such as throw blankets and end tables.

BOTTOM RIGHT Paint open shelves in bright colors to play up your dish displays.

Chapter 8

Getting It Done

Now that you have immersed yourself in the new cottage style, you may be ready to embark on changes in your own space. Whether they are vague or concrete, you probably have some ideas percolating about what you'd like to do. The information in this chapter will help you organize your ideas and institute some quick fixes. It will also help you figure out whether you want to do the work yourself or hire a decorator, and provide key shopping tips for buying vintage.

Use unifying elements like a rug, light fixture, and monochromatic color scheme to give a room a finished look.

B efore you begin, get your ideas organized. Gather all your inspirational and reference materials. Start a file of photos, a wish list of furnishings you like, stores to visit, and names of professionals you wish to consult. You may find a basic manila folder adequate for this material; otherwise, use a loose-leaf notebook with plastic sleeves for photos and sections for each room. An accordion file is useful for things like paint samples and fabric swatches.

ABOVE LEFT Devise a plan for hanging art with disparate pictures unified by similar frames.

TOP RIGHT A few carefully chosen accents provide bold color and texture.

BOTTOM RIGHT Cottage rooms are brightened with soft neutrals and lots of natural light.

OPPOSITE PAGE Give your entryway a cottage feel with paneled and painted wood, a storage bench, and utilitarian hooks.

Assessing Your Space

As you review your materials, figure out how large a project you'd like to take on. Are you looking to redo your entire living space or just one room? Are you searching for colorful accessories to enliven your space? Does your furniture seem heavy or outdated? Are you ready to rethink your color scheme? Figure out the scope of your project and prioritize each phase.

ABOVE If your bedroom lacks a focal point, consider creating a gallery wall with casually displayed pictures.

LEFT One oversized piece—be it framed artwork or a pretty mirror—can provide a finished look and make the space appear larger.

OPPOSITE PAGE Cottage-style elements like white beadboard walls, natural wood, and textural baskets work together to harmonize the room.

Casual whimsy is the
essence of cottage
style. Here, a fanciful
textural frame
achieves a playful pop
against a white wall,
and an old paneled
door is spruced up
with wallpaper.

Quick Updates

If you'd like to freshen your space but aren't sure what changes to make, here are some suggestions for easily infusing cottage charm. A fresh coat of neutral paint in any room will lighten and brighten the space enormously. In the living room, have new slipcovers made for your sofa or drape it in vintage linens and sheepskins for a cozier look and feel. Layer new area rugs on your floor to better define the space. Find a large vintage mirror or gilded picture frame to lean against the mantel or hang above a console. Remove your kitchen cabinet facings and paint the insides glossy white. Paint your bedroom floors white or off-white and layer them with textural rugs. Install wainscoting in the bathroom.

RIGHT Adding white paneling and trim around the tub, a display of decorative glass, and fresh flowers creates cottage style in an existing bathroom.

BOTTOM LEFT To add texture and interest, combine warm wood with a hint of something crystal or gilded.

BOTTOM RIGHT Whether in the living room or kitchen, casually styled open shelves evoke casual cottage charm.

DESIGNER PAULA SMAIL ON

How to Start From Scratch

A room is like a blank canvas. You can start with a color you love, a piece of furniture, or a rug. Build from there but don't get locked into buying certain things first. You might see dining room chairs that will change the way you think about the table. Don't be too rigid. You *can* take detours.

A wood floor, white walls, and softly layered neutrals give this bedroom fresh cottage style.

A fanciful lighting fixture, woven bar stools, and an antique book-rack warm up this kitchen.

Shopping Tips

Check out flea
markets and garage
sales for that one
perfect vintage chair
or painting.

Once you've determined the scope and content of your project, no doubt it will be time to do some shopping. Before you hit the stores, make sure you are properly armed with all necessary measurements of your space and keep a tape measure with you when you go out shopping.

Buying Vintage

One or two vintage pieces can add just the right note of cottage style. Where to find these gems? Blogger Mina Brinkey suggests flea markets, thrift shops, and garage sales for vintage finds at good prices; vintage boutiques, she says, "will generally be more expensive."

Be cautious in your purchases, Brinkey recommends. Look at the bones of the piece and make sure a sofa, chair or table is sturdy and made of solid wood. Also, "look around the piece for dust on the floor," Brinkey advises. "Little tiny wood chips would signify termites, and you want to stay away from those pieces." Finally, try out a sofa or chair to see if it's comfortable, and check it for stains and scratches. Remember, chairs and couches can be reupholstered and given new life. "Look at the potential of the piece and not just the piece itself. Imagination is key," she notes.

As for vintage lighting fixtures, "I highly recommend rewiring any lighting fixture, even if it works, for safety reasons," says Brinkey. Most vintage linens will have some yellowing or stains, so check them out before you purchase. Any item advertised as sterling silver should be engraved to that effect.

When it comes to budgeting, most experts on our panel recommend investing in "anchor" pieces like the sofa, dining table, or bed. Spend less money on accessories, they recommend, as you may tire of them sooner.

LEFT Even without candles, a cluster of beautifully worn candlesticks can give your space a sense of history.

TOP RIGHT When displayed together, a vintage mirror, table, and bowl dress up a cottage entryway.

BOTTOM RIGHT When shopping for vintage armoires, worn wood with patina is a plus. Ensure the piece is solid and sturdy before you buy it.

Hiring a Professional

Experimentation is essential in creating cottage rooms. Bring in lots of texture as you choose materials, and change out displays frequently.

Because cottage style is personal and casual, it is not necessary to hire a professional to achieve it. However, if you would like some extra help, know that interior designers vary in terms of their education, training, and how they work. An interior decorator may or may not have been formally trained and will work with you to choose color palettes, furnishings, fabrics, and lighting for your house.

An interior designer or interior architect will have more formal training and education. These professionals are knowledgeable about architecture and construction and can help you change structural aspects of your house, including exterior elements like windows and doors. Some designers work by the hour; others take a percentage of the overall project budget or a flat fee. Licensed designers should be able to get a trade discount on furnishings. Make sure to look at portfolios and get references before you sign on with a professional.

ABOVE A decorator can help you choose—and coordinate—colors, fabrics, and furnishings for a whole house or just one room.

RIGHT The cozier your room feels, the more inviting it will look, so keep personal comfort in mind when styling your space.

Resources

The following are websites, organizations, manufacturers, retailers, and flea markets mentioned in this book along with a variety of other resources you might find helpful and/or inspirational in your quest for cottage style.

Websites and Blogs

A Beach Cottage: Life by the Sea
www.abeachcottage.com
Decorating inspiration from an Australian design blogger. Includes home tours and room makeovers incorporating vintage finds.

Apartment Therapy
www.apartmenttherpapy.com
A home decorating guide for urban dwellers. Includes product reviews, home tours, and small-space living advice.

Decor8
www.decor8.com
Inspiration for decorating and furnishing your space from stylist Holly Becker.

Design Sponge
www.designsponge.com
Home design inspiration with an emphasis on budget style, DIY, and city living.

Remodelista
www.remodelista.com
Decorating inspiration with a warm, modern feel.

sfgirlbybay
www.sfgirlbybay.com
Home design with vintage style.

Organizations and Associations

American Institute of Architects
www.aia.org

American Society of Interior Designers
www.asid.org

Flea Markets

Alameda Flea Market
Alameda, California
alamedapointantiquesfaire.com
Northern California's largest flea market takes place the first Sunday of the month.

Brimfield Antique Show and Market
Brimfield, Massachusetts
www.brimfieldshow.com
The largest outdoor antique show in the United States hosts three Tuesday-through-Sunday shows each May, July, and September.

Brooklyn Flea: Greenpoint Outdoor Market
Brooklyn, New York
www.brooklynflea.com
This popular flea market takes place at the flagship outdoor location in Fort Greene from April through Thanksgiving.

Daytona Flea & Farmers Market
Daytona Beach, Florida
www.daytonafleamarket.com
The year-round Daytona Flea & Farmers Market in Daytona Beach, Florida, takes place each Friday through Sunday.

First Monday Trade Days
Canton, Texas
www.firstmondaycanton.com
Open Thursday through Sunday prior to the first Monday of each month, about an hour's drive from Dallas.

Greenflea Market in Manhattan
New York City
www.greenfleamarkets.com
Takes place on the upper west side of Manhattan every Sunday. Proceeds benefit two New York City schools.

Long Beach Outdoor Antique and Collectible Market
Long Beach, California
www.longbeachantiquemarket.com
Held on the third Sunday of each month in Veterans Stadium, this year-round outdoor market has more than 800 sellers.

Rose Bowl Flea Market
Pasadena, California
www.rgcshows.com/RoseBowl
This Southern California legend takes place on the second Sunday of every month.

Shipshewana Auction & Flea Market
Shipshewana, Indiana
http://tradingplaceamerica.com/fleamarket.php
The Midwest's largest outdoor flea market takes place Tuesdays and Wednesdays from May through October.

Springfield Antique Show and Flea Market
Springfield, Ohio
www.springfieldantiqueshow.com
Takes place every third full weekend except in June, July, and December.

Retailers and Manufacturers

Adagio
www.adagiosinks.com
Handcrafted sinks, including farmhouse sinks made of wood or carved from natural stone.

Aga
www.aga-ranges.com
A British company known for its classic enameled cast-iron ranges.

Anthropologie

www.anthropologie.com

A women's clothing boutique that also sells one-of-a-kind linens and housewares.

Antique Stoves

www.antiquestove.com

Online retailer of classic vintage stoves.

Carlisle Wide Plank Floors

www.wideplankflooring.com

Maker of historical-style wood flooring in a variety of hardwoods and reclaimed woods.

Clawfoot Supply

www.clawfootsupply.com

Purveyors of vintage claw-foot tubs and accessories.

The Company Store

www.thecompanystore.com

Sells all-natural bedding.

The Container Store

www.containerstore.com

Sells attractive organizing solutions, including decorative baskets and boxes in all sizes.

Flora Grubb

www.floragrubb.com

Purveyor of native California plants, stylish outdoor furnishings, and garden accessories.

Hable Construction

www.hableconstruction.com

Upscale purveyor of fabric storage containers and accessories.

The Home Depot

www.homedepot.com

Ikea

www.ikea.com

Global retailer specializing in affordable, assemble-your-own pieces and colorful accessories.

Lowe's

www.lowes.com

Old Fashioned Milk Paint Company

www.milkpaint.com

Maker of chemically safe, historically accurate paint.

Pottery Barn

www.potterybarn.com

Home retailer selling farmhouse-style tables and furnishings, slipcovers, dishes, and accessories.

Restoration Hardware

www.restorationhardware.com

Retailer of furnishings and lighting fixtures.

Shabby Chic

www.shabbychic.com

Retailers of cottage-style furnishings and linens.

Smeg Appliances

www.smegusa.com

Manufacturers of vintage-style refrigerators.

Trestlewood

www.trestlewood.com

Dealers in reclaimed wood planks and beams.

Vermont Soapstone

www.vermontsoapstone.com

Renowned miners of soapstone and makers of countertops, sinks, and more.

West Elm

www.westelm.com

Casual, affordable furnishings and accessories with a contemporary bent.

The Woods Company

www.thewoodscompany.com

Manufactures flooring from antique wood.

Photography Credits

Melanie Acevedo/Getty Images: 167 bottom, 176 top; Jean Allsopp: 5; Photoshot/Red Cover/Steve Back: 113 top right; Photoshot/Red Cover/James Balston: 138; Edmund Barr: 78 (architect: Beverley Spears, Spears Architects), 153 top (architect: Ellis A. Schoichet, EASA Architecture; design: Bess Wiersema, Megan Matthews, Studio 3 Design); Richard Birch/acpsyndication.com/JBG Photo: 24; Carolyn Borlenghi-Harris: 4; Nick Bowers/acpsyndication.com/JBG Photo: 164 bottom left; Hallie Burton/acpsyndication.com/JBG Photo: 175 top left, 182; Jason Busch/acpsyndication.com/JBG Photo: 27, 82 top left; Sharyn Cairns: 146, 154; Sharyn Cairns/acpsyndication.com/JBG Photo: 57 top right; Photoshot/Red Cover/Alun Callender: 150, Back cover bottom right; Chi-Lin Chien Sun: 5; Lisa Cohen/Taverne Agency: 101, 134; Jonn Coolidge: 88, 108 top left; Daley + Gross: 60 top; davidduncanlivingston.com: 43 bottom right; Roger Davies: 43 top left (kitchen design: Ajax Daniels; house design: Mark Billy); Erica George Dines: 4; Frederic Ducout/Living Inside: 22; John Dummer/Taverne Agency: 96, 97 top right, 97 top left, 133 bottom right; Hotze Eisma/Taverne Agency: 82 top right, 85 top right, 94 top right; Photoshot/Red Cover/Lauren Floodgate: 155 top left; Jared Fowler/acpsyndication.com/JBG Photo: 52 top; James Geer/acpsyndication.com/JBG Photo: 42; Tria Giovan: 8 bottom right, 9, 25, 26, 69, 125 top right, 129 right, 142, 171 bottom right; Photoshot/Red Cover/Tria Giovan: 143 left; Thayer Allyson Gowdy: 74 bottom left, 113 left, 147 bottom, 155 bottom right; John Granen: Front flap (design: J.A.S. Design-Build), 31, 36 left (design: Kevin Price, J.A.S. Design-Build), 36 right (design: Kevin Price, J.A.S. Design-Build), 41 bottom (design: Erik Barr, Urban Wedge), 46 (design: Kevin Price and Kim Clements, J.A.S. Design-Build), 49 (design: Joe Schneider and Kim Clements, J.A.S. Design-Build), 131 top (design: J.A.S. Design-Build); Simon Griffiths/Living

Inside: 132; Photoshot/Red Cover/Winfried Heinze: 13, 105 top; Photoshot/Red Cover/Sarah Hogan: 155 top right; Maree Homer/acpsyndication.com/JBG Photo: 64 bottom, 139 top left, 139 top right, 157, 159, 165; Marjon Hoogervorst: 137; Marjon Hoogervorst/Taverne Agency: 169 bottom; Matthew Hranek/Art + Commerce: 115 top; Bjarni B. Jacobsen/Pure Public/Living Inside: 18 top, 35, 39 right, 57 bottom left, 86 top right, 91, 94 bottom right, 99, 108 bottom, 170, 173, 180, 183 bottom right; Johner Royalty-Free/Getty Images: 64 top, back cover top; Richard Leo Johnson: 44–45; James Knowler/acpsyndication.com/JBG Photo: 176 bottom; Nathalie Krag/Taverne Agency: 38, 43 top right, 124, 162–163; Ben Lambers/Taverne Agency: 74 top left, 141 bottom; Geoff Lung/f8 photo library: 39 left, 55 bottom, 151, 167 top; Joanna Maclennan/Living Inside: 85 left; Per Magnus Persson/Corbis: 185 bottom; Photoshot/Red Cover/Simon McBride: 47 top (design: Veere Grenney); Ericka McConnell: 81 top (styling: Miranda Jones; design: Lillian Mitchell, Harp Ostroy Mitchell Structures), 152 (styling: Philippine Scali; Hideaway Storage Boxes by Hable Construction, www.hablecon struction.com; bedding by Erika Tanov, www.ericatanov.com); Photoshot/Red Cover/Stuart McIntyre: 111 top; Stuart McIntyre/Pure Public/Living Inside: 62, 80, 82 bottom; Anastassios Mentis/Getty Images: 184; Photoshot/Red Cover/N. Minh & J. Wass: 171 top right; Minh + Wass: 11 bottom (design: Daniel Jasiak), 19 (design: Hutker Architects), 23 (design: Daniel Jasiak); Ngoc Minh Ngo: 149 bottom; Ngoc Minh Ngo/Taverne Agency: 179 top; Laura Moss: 8 top (architect and designer: Schappacherwhite LTD), 8 bottom left, 12–13, 20, 21 (stylist: Jessica Thomas), 32, 48 bottom, 63 top (architect and designer: Schappacherwhite LTD), 73 top (architect and designer: Schappacherwhite LTD), 74–75,

87, 102, 103 top, 105 bottom, 111 bottom right, 112 (interior designer: Carey Karlan) 128 (architect and designer: Schappacherwhite LTD), 133 top right, 161 (stylist: Matthew Mead), 169 top (architect and designer: Schappacherwhite LTD); Photoshot/Red Cover/Sophie Munro: 17 top; J. D. Peterson: 47 bottom (architect: Buttrick/Wong Architects); Damien Pleming/acp syndication.com/JBG Photo: 174; Richard Powers: 56, 94 bottom left, 104, 108 top right; Richard Powers/www.sarahkaye.com: 92; Photoshot/Red Cover/Practical Pictures: 149 top; Amanda Prior/acpsyndication.com/JBG Photo: 121; Robert Reichenfeld/acp syndication.com/JBG Photo: 89 top right, 156; Laura Resen: 7, 11 top, 15, 34 top, 51 bottom, 65, 72, 81 bottom, 103 bottom, 107 top, 116 top, 116 bottom, 118–119, 119, 123, 145, 166–167; Lisa Romerein: 28, 29 top left, 29 top right, 29 bottom, 50 (design: Arciform), 53 (architect: David Arkin & Anni Tilt, Arkin Tilt Architects), 61 (design: Roy McMakin), 67 (design: Arciform), 110–111 (architectural design: Julie Hart), 133 top left (design: Arciform), 164 bottom right (architectural design: Julie Hart), 185 top (architectural design: Julie Hart); Lisa Romerein/Getty Images: 168; Eric Roth: 57 bottom right; Prue Ruscoe/acp syndication.com/JBG Photo: 16, 33, 37, 113 bottom right, 163, 177; Prue Ruscoe/Taverne Agency: 63 bottom, 84, 94 top left, 95; Annie Schlechter: 48 top right; Photoshot/Red Cover/Keith Scott: 164 top left; TJ Scott: 5; Rob Shaw/acpsyndication.com/JBG Photo: 120 top left; Michael Skott: 40, 59; Martin Sølyst/erikbjorn.dk/Living Inside: 89 left, 97 bottom right, 98; Thomas J. Story: Front cover, 34 bottom (architect: Neal Schwartz), 41 top (design: Francesca Quagliata, 4th Street Design), 52 bottom right, 57 top left (design: Francesca Harris, FHIG), 58 (architect: David S. Gast & Associates), 60 bottom, 68 left, 77, 79, 90 top, 125 bottom right (architect: Feldman Architecture), 126 top (design: Charles de Lisle,

Your Space Interiors; architect: Heidi Richardson, Richardson Architects), 127 (architect: Levy Art & Architecture), 130, 131 bottom right, 136 left, 136 right (design: Charles de Lisle, Your Space Interiors; architect: Heidi Richardson, Richardson Architects), 140 (design: Dirk Stennick Design), 141 top, 143 right (architect: Levy Art & Architecture), 175 top right (design: Pamela Hill & Lois MacKenzie, Otto Baat Group), 178 (styling: Miranda Jones), 183 top (design: Dirk Stennick Design; lighting and furniture: Jacqueline Bucelli Designs; colors and finishes: Patty Glikbarg, Pannagan Designs), 187, 189, back cover middle, back cover bottom left; Tim Street-Porter: 10, 51 top, 52 bottom left, 55 top, 73 bottom, 109, 114, 115 bottom, 117, 125 left, 126 bottom; Karina Tengberg/Taverne Agency: 85 bottom right; Photoshot/Red Cover/Debi Trelor: 76; Chris Tubbs: 68 right (design: Maiden); Photoshot/Red Cover/Chris Tubbs: 148; Photoshot/Red Cover/Andrew Twort: 131 bottom left; Alexander Van Berge/Taverne Agency: 54, 66, 93; Mikkel Vang/Taverne Agency: 71, 86 bottom, 89 bottom right, 107 bottom, 129 left, 135 top, 153 bottom, 183 bottom left; Dominique Vorillon/Getty Images: 160; Bjorn Wallander: 106–107, 179 bottom right; Chris Warnes/acpsyndication.com/JBG Photo: 1, 83, 111 bottom left, 120 top right, 120 bottom, 135 bottom left, 175 bottom right; Julian Wass: 18 bottom; Simon Watson/Getty Images: 164 top right; Wendell Webber/Botanica/Jupiterimages: 139 bottom; Michael Wee: 147 top; Sarah Wert: 4; Photoshot/Red Cover/Deborah Whitlaw-Llewellyn LLC: 14, 171 left; Michele Lee Willson: 48 top left (design: Brian Eby); Polly Wreford/www.sarahkaye.com: 17 bottom, 133 bottom left; Photoshot/Red Cover/Mel Yates: 135 bottom right; Hans Zeegers/Taverne Agency: 86 top left, 90 bottom, 179 bottom left

Index

Sunset guides you to a fabulous home—inside and out

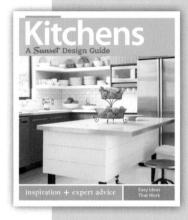

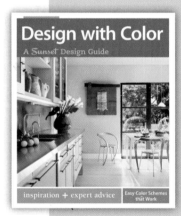

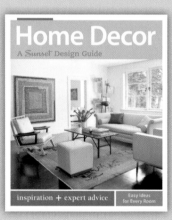

Sunset's all-new Design Guides have everything you need to plan—and create—the home of your dreams. Each book includes advice from top professionals and hundreds of illustrative photos. With an emphasis on green building materials and techniques, this entire series will inspire ideas both inside and outside of your home.